S0-BBX-885

Dec 23

GETTING IT

The Psychology of est

GETTING IT

The Psychology of est

DR. SHERIDAN FENWICK

J. B. Lippincott Company
PHILADELPHIA AND NEW YORK

Copyright © 1976 by Sheridan Fenwick
All rights reserved
First edition

Printed in the United States of America

U.S. Library of Congress Cataloging in Publication Data

Fenwick, Sheridan, birth date
  Getting it: the psychology of est.

  Includes bibliographical references.
  1. Erhard seminars training.   I. Title.
RC489.E7F46   158   76–20617
ISBN–0–397–01170–9

To Murray

Contents

Acknowledgments

I'd like to thank:

George and Ingrid, for the dinner conversation which started this;

Joel, for clearing things up in the process of lunch itself;

Jesse, for sharing his view of what really is;

Bob, for generosity;

Bert, for leveling at the Luna;

Janet H. and Robert T., for being the source;

Mel, for total professionalism;

Beatrice, for talent and tact;

Murray, for everything.

Part I:

THE TRAINING

1

The Reason Why

ONE FALL EVENING at a country inn, I had dinner with an old friend and two new acquaintances. Conversation was relaxed and drifting. At about the time the second course was due to arrive, George mentioned the est training. He and Ingrid and Joel had all been through the training and were smiling with a sense of camaraderie. I lost interest in my onion soup and became totally absorbed in their enthusiasm. They each, without a doubt, appeared sure that the training had been worthwhile. I wasn't sure why. I remember that somebody talked of being able to communicate in a more satisfying way. There were several anecdotes about life going unusually well—career breakthroughs, a sense of satisfaction with the flow of daily events.

Although I am a trained clinical psychologist, I have nevertheless managed to avoid all the "consciousness" movements on the contemporary scene. I thought *those* things were superficial and inauthentic. I had never been into T-groups, TA, TM, Esalen, Arica, Gestalt, Mind Dynamics, or Sufi weekends. The only primal scream I had ever uttered was when I broke my ankle in a hopscotch tournament in seventh grade. For me, a meaningful encounter meant running into somebody I hadn't seen in a long time. My own clinical training was rigorous, conservative, and psychoanalytically oriented. In my research and teaching I ignored the fast-food therapeutic establishments, except when I needed to tell a joke to wake up students who were falling asleep in class. I thought of myself as a *serious* scientist.

Then I began to meet est graduates. They gave uniformly glowing testimonials about the value they had received from the est training. Something made them seem different from the usual self-improvement seekers I had known. I wasn't at all sure what it was that distinguished them. Maybe it had something to do with their apparent self-confidence; they didn't seem like people who were desperate about life. There was none of the false sentimentality I had come to associate with encounter-group addicts. One of the most appealing things of all was that none of them ever volunteered suggestions on how I ought to change my life.

I wasn't looking for miracles. I wasn't even particularly interested in the specifics of what someone "got" from the est training. It was definitely style rather than substance that appealed to me: a contentment that transcended complacency. The est graduates spoke of satisfaction and aliveness and seemed to enjoy life.

My talks with these graduates coincided with a period in my professional life when I was becoming interested in alternatives to traditional psychotherapy, a search which in turn reflected the ferment within the traditional mental health establishment as it recognized the need for shorter, less expensive forms of treatment. I was curious about all the informal ways in which people handle problems and conflicts, discover a sense of meaning or purpose in their lives, and sometimes seem to find *joie de vivre*.

So I considered doing est. I was curious about it. I also thought the experience might suggest some ideas for research.

I began to look for information about the program. It was no small-time operation. By the end of 1975 more than 70,000 people had directly and intensively participated in it, and the number of est graduates had doubled each year since its founding in 1971. The est organization conducted trainings in twelve cities: Aspen, Berkeley/Oakland, Boston, Chicago, Denver, Honolulu, Los Angeles, New York, San Diego, San Francisco, San Jose, and Washington, D.C. Plans for expansion were reported in the media. They had trained children as young as six years of age. There was a special two-week wilderness program for teenagers. Trainings had been conducted in public schools in California and in a prison. There were special workshops for educators, psychotherapists, health professionals, and members of the media. Founder Werner Erhard said in an interview that he wanted to train the police.

It was a lot easier to find out these things about est than it was to get any details on what the training was about. (Trainees are in fact requested not to reveal to nongraduates the contents of the est training, although they are encouraged to "share their *experience*.") So I resolved to take the training, not as a professional observer but as a participant, attempting as far as possible to hold in abeyance any critical analysis. That, I thought, could come later, based on extensive notes of my own reactions that I would record at night when I returned home from each session.

I took the training. It was an extraordinary experience. And I have some serious concerns about the implications of the est phenomenon. I think people ought to know about it. I think people ought to *think* about it.

What follows is a detailed description of the est training as I experienced it.

2
Preliminaries

IT WAS EARLY OCTOBER when I decided to do it. I called the est office in New York and said I wanted to sign up as soon as possible. The next available training would start the beginning of December. It would be conducted in a slightly different manner from the usual two-weekend seminars. The Pre-Training Seminar would be held one night about a week ahead. We would begin the first half of the training at 7 P.M. Monday and continue "until finished," meeting again on Tuesday, Wednesday, and Thursday nights. The second half of the training would take place on Saturday and Sunday a week later.

In that first phone conversation, the volunteer on the other end of the line asked my name and address and told me about the $30 nonrefundable deposit. He went out of his way to make sure I understood I wouldn't get the money back if I changed my mind

17

about enrolling in the training. As I was ready to hang up the phone, he asked if I had any questions. I disappointed him.

Within a day the first envelope from est was in my mailbox. They soon sent a preliminary schedule for the training and a questionnaire which had the usual questions about age and occupation and a few others specific to est. They asked what one's objective was in taking the est training and then what specific results you hoped to accomplish through the training. My answer to the first was that I merely wanted to experience it; to the question about specific results I replied "none."

The last part of the questionnaire was about experience in psychotherapy, accompanied by a straightforward statement that est was not psychotherapeutic in nature. They asked if one were currently in therapy or had been within the last six months. Then they inquired, for those in therapy now or recently, whether you were "winning"—that is, whether therapy was "handling" those things you were in therapy for. I was impressed with the caution they seemed to take. I had heard from a psychiatrist colleague that they discouraged people with prior psychiatric hospitalizations from taking the training; they also discouraged patients who were not "winning." For those who were successfully in therapy, the questionnaire noted that one's therapist must be informed of the est training because they did not wish to provide any "inputs" that the therapist would be unaware of.

Several weeks later a final schedule for the training arrived and then shortly afterward a phone call from the est office. It was someone identifying himself as Art and saying that one of my answers on the questionnaire was unacceptable. They didn't like it if you had no specific results in mind. Art explained that "you get from the training whatever you put down," so you have to put down something. I didn't have anything in mind, so I asked him for some suggestions. I felt like a child asking the department store Santa Claus for a rundown on what was in stock this year. Art told me that other people said things like they'd like to be less anxious, or they'd like to solve some particular problem in their life, or they'd like to clear up a relationship with a friend. He said that one of his desires before he took the training was to be able to survive the first day without smoking, and— funny thing—he had mysteriously, without effort or plans, stopped just two weeks before the training. I was not particularly inspired by any of the wishes he had suggested, so I said I'd think about it and come up with something by the time of the Pre-Training Seminar. He also reminded me that the rest of the fee—$220—was due within a week.

I sent the second check with greater reluctance than I had mailed the first. I was beginning to think that the experience was not going to be something I'd feel like paying for.

The Pre-Training Seminar was held at a mid-town hotel on the Tuesday night before the training was to start. As I walked into the lobby by myself, a man standing just inside the door motioned me down the hall and to my left. I wondered how he knew where I was going. At the entrance to the corridor was a cardboard sign, propped on an easel, stating that this was an est "private meeting." I walked into the ballroom lobby and saw long lines of people waiting to be helped by est volunteers, seated behind an array of tables. Someone said that the lines were being formed alphabetically, but it was almost impossible to tell which letters were supposed to go where. I finally walked to the front of one of the lines and asked a volunteer for the F's. It was the line right next to me and fortunately the shortest one around.

There were name tags on the table, and the volunteer had a notebook containing the application questionnaires. When my turn came at the head of the line I immediately spotted my name tag on the table, but it was clear that there was business to be done before I could take possession of it. She looked up my questionnaire in her notebook and carefully read over it to see that all was complete. When she got to the results question she frowned, looked up at me, and repeated the question. I was ready for her. "I'd like to clear up a relationship with a friend," I said, partly because it was true and partly because it was the most innocuous "result" that had been suggested to me over the phone.

She seemed to like it, smiled, and said, "That's fine. Write it in." After I complied, I was awarded a tag with my first name in large black letters and my last name in small print underneath.

I walked toward the doors of the room where the session was to be held, struggling to take off my coat and holding my name tag in my hand. There were more volunteers at the door. "Please put your name tag on before entering the room." I was annoyed at that; it was obvious I was trying to take my coat off. But I knew this would only be the beginning of a series of rules, so I tried not to find it irritating.

Inside the hotel ballroom hundreds of chairs were lined up in front of a stage, as though for a meeting. Volunteers were ushering people into seats. It seemed as though almost everybody was still outside, dealing with questionnaires and name tags. The chairs were so close together there was no room to move at all, and coats and belongings were clearly in the way. The room was only partially filled by the hundred people or so who filed into place and sat silently, waiting.

At seven fifteen, the scheduled starting time, someone walked onto the stage and did a military right-face when he reached the center. His voice was chilling. "Good evening. There will be a delay in starting due to the large number of people who have not completed their paperwork. We will begin promptly at seven thirty, which is fourteen minutes from now. Thank you." And he was gone. He gave me the creeps. I hoped he wouldn't be in charge of the evening.

Things began in exactly fourteen minutes. The room was full by then and still strangely silent. Another man walked onto the stage and introduced himself as Ken,* the leader of the Pre-Training Seminar. He seemed more human than the first man, more relaxed, with an occasional smile. He began by going over the schedule for the training. I was instantly bored, having read the schedule several times in the material that had been mailed to me and seen it written on the blackboards standing on either side of the stage. I wondered if the seminar would continue at such a tedious pace.

It did. The next hour and a half was mainly a repetition of the rules and suggestions that had been noted on the questionnaire. The information for people in therapy was given with emphasis. The rules for the training were described: Arrive promptly; no one will leave the room until a break is announced; no

---

* To protect the privacy of all persons involved in the training I have used fictitious names for the trainers and the trainees mentioned in my account of the est experience.

reading, sewing, or other busywork allowed in the training room; no note-taking; no smoking, eating, or going to the bathroom except during an announced break. For the two weeks surrounding the training period, no alcohol was to be consumed and no drugs or other substances used for the purpose of altering one's consciousness were to be taken. Medications identified as essential by one's physician were allowed; birth-control pills were permissible. People with medical problems requiring exceptions to these rules would inform an official at the first training session and would be seated in a special section where their needs could be attended to. If you knew anyone else in the room before you came to the training, you were requested not to sit near them. The leader announced that no justification for the rules would be offered, since the rationale was the same for all of them: They worked. However, he was willing to take questions if someone needed clarification of what they meant. He avoided calling them rules; the accepted jargon was "agreements." There were a few questions from the audience. Several people seemed to find it difficult to believe that "no alcohol" *really* meant to exclude wine with dinner.

Then we were instructed to walk around the room and meet each other. The leader demonstrated how we were to behave by parodying the typical sidewalk encounter of acquaintances where neither person ever looks directly at the other. We, on the contrary, would be looking people in the eye and introducing ourselves. All 250 of us got up at the signal and began milling. It was a standard sensitivity-encounter-group exercise, mildly interesting for the first few minutes and then tiresome. It seemed as if I met all 249 other fellow trainees, as well as most of the volunteer staff, who were standing like monitors in the back of the room. Soon it was absolutely mechanical to reach for someone's hand, shake it while looking him or her in the eye, and say "Hi, I'm Sheri." After hearing that person's name I'd add, just as the leader had shown me, "It's nice to meet you. Thank you." It had gotten to the point where I was meeting the same people over and over when finally the end of the exercise was proclaimed. We sat down again for a few more minutes of instruction, and then a break was announced.

I was grateful for the ice water at the back of the room and then realized how much I wanted a cigarette. I had to go to the lobby for that, so I made my way through the crowd and quickly stationed myself next to one of the few available ashtrays. I looked around at my fellow trainees in the lobby. The group ranged in age from about twenty to maybe seventy. More than half seemed to be under thirty-five or forty. All were well dressed, clearly middle class, and outwardly successful in life. My observations were interrupted by a friendly voice asking if I was married and if my husband approved of my taking the est training. The inquirer was a man in his early forties who told me that his wife thought the whole enterprise was silly and a waste of time. We talked for another ten minutes or so, somehow discovering that we both shared the opinion that the Connecticut Berkshires were the best place for quick weekend escapes from New York City. Then I left to find a ladies' room before the session resumed. I had missed the bathroom rush at the start of the break but was now faced with a total absence of supplies. I quickly calculated that 250 people paying $250 apiece were providing the est organization with $62,500 for this training. I thought that for $62,500 they could at least make sure there was toilet paper.

Everyone else had returned to the meeting room early, and I was ushered into a seat farther back from the stage than my original one. I felt much more engulfed by the crowd. Some more instructions were given about the training, and then the leader helped us organize into carpools for our trips home. Some people had come from relatively far away, suburbs that were more than an hour and a half out of the city. I raised my hand for the Upper West Side and noted the corner of the room where we were instructed to get together afterward with others who would share a cab uptown.

Finally we began to do something that seemed at

least vaguely justifiable as "training." Ken told us to put our feet firmly on the floor, clear our laps of coats, pocketbooks, and other possessions, take off our glasses, and sit quietly with our eyes closed. He then began to chant instructions: "Put your consciousness and awareness into your feet. Create a space for your feet. Put your consciousness and awareness into your ankles. Put your consciousness and awareness into your legs . . . your buttocks . . . your stomach . . . your chest . . . your lungs . . . your heart . . . your back . . . your head. Recall a beach. Put your consciousness and awareness into the beach. Look out at the horizon and see the color of the sky and of the water. Look down the beach to your right. Look right down there and notice what you see. Look down the beach to your left. Feel the spray of water on your cheeks. Maybe there are some gulls flying by. Experience the beach. Put your consciousness and awareness into the beach. Now recall a time when you were happy. . . . Recall a time when you felt strong. . . . Recall a time when life was cheerful. . . . Recall a time when you felt good. . . . Recall something red from yesterday. . . ."

The chant was seemingly endless. I felt very relaxed. Finally Ken told us to come back to the room gradually and open our eyes slowly. When I looked around, I felt as though I had been away for a long time.

The culmination of the evening focused on what est calls "Personality Profiles." Cards were given out, on which we were told to put the name and city or town of someone we knew who was not in the room. We then listed the person's sex, age, height, weight, and marital status; three adjectives describing the person's personality; three situations or things to which the person would react and a description of these reactions; and three more people (by name and their relationship to the person whose profile we were writing) and a description of the person's reaction to each of these other people. The cards were collected and we were told they would be destroyed after this evening. I didn't believe that.

An est graduate named Debbie was introduced and invited to take a place on the stage. Her entrance was greeted with applause, started by Ken and quickly picked up by the audience. Ken then picked a card from the pile and asked the person who had written it to join them. The writer was a young girl who looked like a college student. Debbie, also a young woman, was instructed by Ken to "create a space." She closed her eyes and seemed to be concentrating. Ken then led her through a series of questions about the person described in the profile, each time asking the writer for confirmation of the accuracy of Debbie's descriptions. Some of the questions were setups: "Do you think this person is intelligent or not intelligent?" I didn't believe anybody would have written a description of someone he or she considered a "not intelligent" person. Other answers were vague enough to apply to almost anyone. The only outright error came in response to a question of the person's reaction to tennis. Debbie thought that the person she was describing would be an enthusiastic tennis player, probably quite good, a real tennis buff. In fact, Debbie could actually "see" her wearing sneakers and those short tennis socks with pompons on the back. The writer contradicted this and stated that her friend in fact hardly played tennis at all and felt frustrated that she didn't have time to. The audience seemed to enjoy this display and applauded loudly.

The trainees were invited to comment on Debbie's performance. One woman thought that Debbie had extrasensory perception. Another woman thought we all could do such predictions if we just put our minds to it, and another said she thought it was just coincidence, like newspaper horoscopes which are general enough to apply to almost anyone. Each commentator was thanked by Ken and the audience applauded politely. I was in a state of mild to moderate outrage. I free-associated: Nonsense . . . where are the control groups? . . . this whole thing is a sham . . . an introductory psychology student could expose this for what it is . . . these people are uninformed and gullible to boot . . . for *this* I paid two hundred and fifty *dollars?* . . . there's a sucker born every minute

. . . you can fool all of the people most of the time
. . . what was it I heard about this guy Erhard having
been an encyclopedia salesman? . . . I hope none of
my colleagues ever finds out I've had anything to do
with this organization . . . do the est people really
think all of us are this dumb? And on and on and on.

We were dismissed shortly after 11 P.M., and I
found a group of people to share a cab home.

3

Your Life Doesn't Work

I ARRIVED AT THE HOTEL on Monday evening about twenty minutes before the session was scheduled to begin and found a seat third row center. It was a different hotel but the same physical layout as before. While I was waiting for things to start, I listened to a few conversations going on around me. In the row in front two young women were playing with a "mood ring," one of those stones that "reveals your innermost feelings." Behind me someone was describing to her neighbor the reactions of people in her family who had already taken the est training. "It saved my sister's marriage; her three children would be in *a broken home* today if Naomi hadn't taken the training. My mother is a different person; we all think so. My father can't believe she's changed so much." Next to her another trainee was wondering out loud if we would be allowed to help each other. "Suppose someone is really going through something heavy, are we allowed to reach out to them?" No one seemed to know what we would be allowed to do. Farther down that aisle from the would-be helper was a woman wearing the yellow badge of an est graduate; she was taking the training for a second time. I missed her explanation of why. A man in my row was a chiropractor and had been told about est by some of his patients. Last month he had gone to an astrologer.

At 7 P.M. a man walked onstage and loudly announced that we would start late to allow people to complete their paperwork. All other sessions would start promptly. Since I didn't have a watch (that was one of the rules) I don't know how long it was before Guido, the training supervisor, reappeared and began dealing with the logistics of the training. He described the procedure for people needing to make special arrangements, such as to take medication or to leave the room during the training. They seemed to take a long time with arrangements and rules and announcements, although they were well organized.

Abruptly our trainer, Stephen, arrived. His voice was less annoying than Guido's. Ground rules were again gone over. This time the est people were willing to recognize them as rules, although they still seemed to enjoy describing them as agreements. We were told that we would have a chance to indicate our agreement to abide by the instructions by returning to the room after the break, which would occur many hours later. Anyone who did not choose to do this could leave at that point, and that person's "tuition" would be returned. (I noticed the similarity to those things that used to come in the mail, telling you that you would be a charter subscriber to a new record club unless they received your card back within a few days refusing the offer. I wondered how long that had been illegal.) Stephen continued with a reiteration of the rules. No watches, clocks, or other timepieces in the training room. No food, not even snacks, candies, or gum. That meant Life Savers too. On breaks that were not specifically described as food breaks, we were to consume only coffee, tea, water, soft drinks, or fruit juices. No milk. No smoking in the training room. No medications that a physician had not told you that you *must* have or must have under certain conditions. Only people who had made arrangements with the training supervisor to have their names placed on the "special permissions list" would be allowed to leave the room at any time other than an announced break. No note-taking. No tape recorders. No reading material in the training room. No talking unless recognized and given permission by the trainer. Questions would be answered when and if the trainer recognized you; an est volunteer would then scuttle down the aisle and pass a microphone to you. (We were at this point given what seemed to be about fifteen minutes of instruction on how to use a microphone.) No discussion of anything other than personal reactions with anyone who was not an est graduate; no revealing of est information, content, or processes to non-est graduates.

Understanding the agreements was the first part of the training and, Stephen added, would *be* the training for some of us. Life doesn't work when agreements are not kept. Part of the reason why we trainees were "assholes" was that we didn't keep our agreements. People actually set themselves up to break agreements, thinking secretly, "Well, that's not fair, so I'm not really bound by it." Stephen had no respect for fairness. He pushed over the stool standing on the stage. "Does it matter whether you think it's fair for this chair to fall? The chair doesn't give a shit. It doesn't matter whether you *believe* in gravity or not. That's just the way it is." Stephen then wheeled around and noted that he knew that some of us were planning to break the agreements; we had watches or gum or snacks in our pockets, just in case. That was the number we always did—keeping one foot in a safety zone, withholding our commitment. We were warned that such lapses in integrity would haunt us, that all our broken agreements would surface during the training. People who were pulling this act were given a chance to go to the back of the room and turn in their contraband. Several people did so.

We were harangued for a long time, with continued demonstrations of our "asshole" status. We were told that our lives didn't work and, what's more, we lied about it. We knew nothing. We were run by our bladders. We were controlled by our problems. We lacked integrity and had no sense of responsibility. We lived in the realm of nonexperience. None of this bothered Stephen, he assured us; he didn't give a shit —he already had our money. That's the way they did it at est; they won first and then played the game.

A motherly woman in the first row was recognized and given a microphone. She said she was annoyed at the use of four-letter words. (I knew that she was referring to "asshole" as a four-letter word.) Stephen said he'd be using more of them and she'd just have to get used to it. Her problem was that she was offended by *words*. After the training, none of us would think "fuck" was any different from "spaghetti." (That comment led to some interesting fantasies on my part.) On the other side of the room someone else was recognized and microphoned; she thought that Stephen was behaving like a bastard to the nice lady in the front row. "Thank you," said Stephen, and he clapped for her. We were given instructions to acknowledge, with applause, any comments made, regardless of our opinions of them. The applause was not a vote, just a simple recognition of message received.

Stephen then began a lecture. The Scale of Knowing was written on the top of one blackboard and the Scale of Experiencing was written on the other. It took hours for Stephen to label the successive points on both scales. In terms of Knowing, he placed most of us at the third rung from the bottom, the level of Belief—symbols, signs, and perceptions. We knew the things we knew because we *believed* them. We were told to suspend belief, even to the extent that we should not believe anything we were being told in the training. (I didn't mind that—intellectual skepticism was just fine with me. I had been rebelling against belief ever since I resigned from Sunday school.) Below Belief on the Scale of Knowing, at the second rung from the bottom, was Mystery—I guessed this was probably what some religious people call "faith." The very bottom of the scale was called Unconsciousness, which I translated to mean the state of sleepwalking that I thought most people existed in. For a long time I had viewed Americans as a population of somnambulists. If you think about it, it wouldn't be hard to figure out that the whole world is asleep.

Above Belief on the Scale of Knowing was Feeling, or emotions. In the est scheme of things, above Feeling was Doing Something About It, or the experimental method. This began to make sense to me, along the lines of "Don't just stand there, *do something!*" These things—Unconsciousness, Mystery, Belief, Feeling, Doing Something About It—were all *below* a line on the Scale of Knowing. I wondered, Whose line is that? Obviously it was Werner Erhard's. We were told that we didn't get to vote on it. I never did find out what the line was supposed to be, but I guessed it represented the beginnings of "enlightenment" or some such concept.

Directly above the line was Observation. This was also referred to as Witnessing and was explained as just taking a (fresh) look at something. It involved suspending one's set of beliefs, assumptions, and implications, and the considerations we held that qualified our statements. It meant operating without all the elaborations which we attached to the simple matters of fact in our lives, the "therefores" that followed events as though there were an inevitability about it all, as in "I've just failed an exam; *therefore* I must be a terrible person," based on the *belief* that people who fail exams are worthless.

Above Observation was a category called Certain That You Know, the ah-ha! phenomenon. Even better than that on the road to enlightenment, or wherever it was we were going, was Certain That You Don't Know. Knowing that you don't know something was clearly a state of enlightenment from my point of view. Conveying a sense of the limits of knowledge was often the major goal of lectures I had given to undergraduate psychology students. It had for a long time seemed true to me that ignorance was rather a state of false knowledge, giving one a deceptive sense of security which rested on the ability to remain uninformed. It had its appeal, that was for

sure; what you don't know can't hurt you, as long as
you know that you don't know it.

At the very top of the Scale of Knowing was something like "certainty" which they called Natural
Knowledge. This concept remained enigmatic despite
Stephen's several minutes of discourse on the topic. We
were told, however, not to worry if we did not quite
grasp it, as it was impossible for us to "get" things
which were "above" us. (I thought I had been keeping
an open mind about most of this, but the suggestion
that part of the est epistemology was "above" me was
infuriating.)

Our instruction in how far away we were from
knowing anything was accompanied by a demonstration of the manner in which we filtered our experience
through our expectations of what things *should* be
like. Stephen wrote on the blackboard:

Paris		A bird
in the	and	in the
the		the
spring		hand

Sure enough, most of the audience did not notice the
repetition of "the" in each phrase.

The Scale of Experiencing, also divided by a line,
was laid out on the other blackboard. Several categories of nonexperienced experience were below the

line. Their distinguishing characteristics were non-aliveness and an automatic, mechanical quality. Of course we were at the bottom rung, at the level of Reasonableness, where we looked for reasons, the causes of things. Stephen told us that understanding was the booby prize in life. Things were beginning to take on a decidedly anti-intellectual cast. I guessed that the people in charge were relatively uneducated and defensive about it. At the same time, I could still make some sense out of most of this and relate it to observations I had made independently. In my profession I could hardly be "against" understanding, but it had occurred to me on more than one occasion that some people use their search for understanding as a way of avoiding life. Reasons become excuses and alibis preclude change. A patient I had worked with in psychotherapy for several years was deciding to terminate therapy. She said she was tired of analyzing her life and ready to start living it. I knew what she meant. I lost a patient but the world gained a participant.

Above Reasonableness on the experience scale was a category called Decisions, the explanation of which I missed because I was thinking of my former patient and wondering how her life was actually going for her these days. Next came the level of Hope, where, we were informed, a lot of us got stuck. I was willing to go along with casting aspersions upon hope, as it had always struck me as being about as useless as regret. We moved up a rung on the scale to the level of Help, which was described as a means of dealing with people in a manner which was designed to keep them wherever they were. I had visions of Lady Bountiful and assumed that we were being told that help was condescension. I remembered that whenever I had called the est office, people always answered the phone by saying, "How may I assist you?" In est terminology, assistance was all right. But Help, Hope, Decisions, and Reasonableness, in descending order, were all below the line. I had stopped being bothered by the apparent arbitrary nature of the line-setting business.

The first step above the line, into the realm of experienced experience, was known as Acceptance. I started to provide my own background music. I could hear, with full stereo effects in the recording studio of my mind, John Lennon and Paul McCartney singing "words of wisdom": Let it be. In the days before I had a personal philosophy of life, I would have thought this was passive, submissive hogwash. I had spent my adolescence in the civil rights movement, followed by the general political radicalization that had been the Zeitgeist of the sixties in America. I knew that if you weren't part of the solution, you were part of the problem. I prided myself on being an Activist, which I viewed as a role demanded of me as a patriotic citizen pledged to defend the United States Constitution, unlike some of the people (most of the people?), who had somehow become ensconced in

Washington, acting fully like closet subversives while mouthing platitudes about law 'n' order as they broke every law that inconvenienced them. I always wanted to Do Something about that. As it turned out, I didn't ever do much. I was too scared. So my fantasies of being this century's Patrick Henry, Thomas Jefferson, and Thomas Paine rolled up into one figure of Mosaic proportions receded into a few letters of mild indignation I carefully composed and mailed to my allegedly elected representatives.

By the time the decade changed digits, I had moved to the country and spent a year sitting under a waterfall. It was a year of total self-indulgence, after many years of hard work and harder thinking. The main thing I indulged was my passion for what I have come to think of fondly as bibliotherapy. I spent months reading literature and philosophy and ultimately, thanks to the guidance of a friend, found what I had been looking for in the writings of Epictetus, Seneca, and Marcus Aurelius. My conversion to Stoicism occurred in the same year that Lennon and McCartney were telling us, "There will be an answer." Let it be. Epictetus had begun his manual for life by noting that there are things which are under our own control and things which are not. Simply put, and it *is* simple, those things which are within our own control are our reactions to events, our opinions, our feelings, our desires and dislikes. Everything else—including material things and the opinions of others—is beyond our control. Happiness and freedom are a function of concerning yourself only with that which is within your own control. As for the rest, be prepared to let them be. The voice of Epictetus has been echoed through generations of psychologists confirming his statement: "Men are disturbed not by things, but by the views which they take of things."

So I no longer thought that Acceptance belonged only to the cultists of fundamentalist religion. I had begun to view it as wisdom. The est commentary on Acceptance ran on in a vein that became increasingly Eastern in philosophy. Stephen warned of the dangers of being *attached* to things. I could again interpret this within a Stoic framework: Disappointment comes from wanting things which are not within your own control. Don't want anything and you'll always get what you want. Of course I never applied this in my own life. Nevertheless, I endorsed it. My inability to practice what I would have preached, had I the occasion or the temerity, was probably related to whatever had kept me away from Eastern philosophies during an era when mysticism was pervading the culture. I was a confirmed Apollonian even when everybody I knew was busy becoming a Dionysian junkie.

Participation was above Acceptance on the Scale of Experiencing. Participation meant sharing. The est message was curiously confusing in this regard. We were encouraged to "share" with one another in the

training by requesting a microphone and testifying to
the wonders that were even now being wrought in our
lives by our experience in the est training. It also
seemed OK with them for people, within the confines
of the training room, to communicate their doubts,
suspicions, and dissatisfactions with the training. These
were of course immediately demolished by the skillful
trainer, who was an adroit Sophist. Sometimes his
counterarguments were soundly rational, but more
often they struck me as a supremely elegant con. So,
"sharing" had its limits. We had of course been specifically instructed not to "share" the content of the
training with non-estians. It was suggested that such
information would only confuse them. (Information
is, of course, never confusing, while obfuscation is designed to be. A month after my training I spoke with
friends who had continued their involvement with the
est organization by taking the graduate seminars,
working at the est office, "assisting" at other trainings,
and participating in an advanced training program for
those who aspired to be leaders of Guest Seminars.
For many of them disillusionment had set in when
they noticed that the est message began to boil down
to one topic, that of communication: What was to be
communicated was the value of taking the est training.
Salesmen for est were being turned out by the thousands, some now so turned around that they were
convinced whenever they enrolled a new potential
trainee that they had done *themselves* a favor. And

maybe they had. At this point in my training, however, "sharing" had not yet deteriorated into selling.)

Next on the Scale of Experiencing was Realization. And at the very top of the list was something they annoyingly called Sourcing, which is est jargon for "being the source" of everything that happens to you. I tolerated the language because we were now being tempted with a list of the goodies life held in store for us when we had completed our training. The est training, we were told, was designed to take us above the line to the level of experienced experience, where our future existences would be characterized by aliveness, natural behavior, spontaneity, responsibility, choice, and being the cause, rather than the effect, of things. I was willing to take a crack at it, but I had trouble ignoring the zombielike faces of the est volunteers who staffed the training room and the True Believer fervor of those who pitched me for the training.

Stephen told us that, despite illusions to the contrary, we didn't know *how* to do *anything*. This was demonstrated by a volunteer from the audience who came up to the stage and tried to tell or show Stephen how he walked. "See," scoffed Stephen, "you don't even know how to walk. You *do it* all the time but you don't even know how." The futility of education was announced.

We went over the purpose of the est training, which had been described in a sentence that had been printed on the first mailing I had received after sending in my deposit: "The purpose of the est training is to transform your ability to experience living so that the situations you have been trying to change or have been putting up with clear up just in the process of life itself." Certain key words were defined for us. Purpose meant the continuous nature of the est training. Transform meant transubstantiate, not merely to alter the appearance of something but to change its very substance. Ability meant power. Experience meant to be with. Living meant the moment. So: the continuous nature of the est training is to change the very substance of your power to be with the moment, a kind of Turn on, Tune in, and Drop your guard.

Several people were called on to state what would constitute "getting it" for them. Some of them had materialistic goals; getting it meant getting rich, or famous, or married. For others, "it" was a change in the behavior of someone else: children, husbands, wives, parents, and friends who were earnestly being desired to shape up. Most people who shared their ideas of "it" were thinking along more psychological lines; they wanted to be less anxious, more comfortable in particular kinds of situations, with more self-confidence and more enthusiasm for life. They wanted to be happy. In each case, Stephen revealed that he could not promise them whatever it was they'd like to see happen, but he *could* guarantee that the training would alter the substance of their ability to experience whatever barriers existed between them and their desires.

Two people in the room shared that they had headaches. The first was asked to hold it until tomorrow night, when the training would "handle" headaches. (I wondered where one "held" a headache.) The second acher was more insistent. She maintained that she *needed* to take an aspirin for her headache and did not understand why she couldn't. She had a headache because she was tired. Stephen asked her how she knew that. She started to say she knew it because she had not gotten much sleep the night before, but Stephen interrupted and asked her to spare us her *reasons* and just describe her experience of being tired. She mentioned her scratchy eyes, her tense shoulder muscles, her thighs aching because she needed to move around. Hold it. No sooner had she muttered the giveaway word "because" than Stephen forcefully reminded her not to give reasons. "Just stay with your experience." This went on for a while and then Stephen thanked her. He asked how her experience of tiredness had changed. On a scale of one to ten, with ten being how tired she was when she had first spoken out about it, she now thought she would be at about five.

There was a point to this, we were told: Completed experiences disappear. Only those we resist continue to bother us. Someone on the other side of the room disliked the idea of good experiences disappearing. That was all right for problems, headaches, and stuff like that, but she wanted to hold onto the good things. Holding onto an experience by not completing it prevents you from creating space for something else, she was told. Ho-hum. I was bored and, even more important than that, I was embarrassed. People seemed to be asking permission to hold onto those things that were of importance to them. Then I felt a sadness that moved me deeply: How desperate we all were, how much like children, and how little it took in the way of promises from authority to make us want to believe in God. I guessed that most of us had not yet completed the process of mourning his death.

The impending break was mentioned, but we still weren't ready for it and the release it would offer. More harangue. Finally, we were told it was half past midnight and we would be allowed half an hour. Before they let us go, Guido came back onstage and told us how to find the bathrooms, repeating the instructions twice for each location. Somehow that stuck in my mind more clearly than most of the est verbiage that I was definitely making an effort to remember: To reach the ladies' room on the lobby level, go out of this room and turn left. Go up two flights of stairs to the lobby and turn left. The registration desk will be facing you. Walk past the coffee shop in the direction of the pizza shop, take another left for as far as you can go, then turn right. It recycled: Go out of this room and turn left. Go up two flights of stairs to the lobby and turn left. The registration desk will be facing you. Walk past the coffee shop in the direction of the pizza shop, take another left for as far as you can go, then turn right.

I went out of the room and turned left. Two flights up, I saw that the coffee shop was closed and walked out the front door, onto Seventh Avenue, to look for a place that was open. It was cold and I dashed down the block to a coffee and doughnut shop. I spotted someone I recognized from the training sitting at the counter and took the stool next to hers as we started to chat about our initial reactions to what had gone down in the training room. This was *not* a food break, so we both maintained our vows and ordered only coffee. I was hungry. Sitting across from us was a man wearing the est name tag and eating a blueberry muffin. He looked over at us sheepishly. I had a clear sense of moral superiority which in retrospect disgusted me. Someone called my name and I spun around in the direction of the caller. Two men at the other end of the counter were leering in my direction, one of them obviously with fine enough eyesight to have read my name tag from a distance. "Are you girlies at some sort of convention?" he asked. I looked at the woman I was sitting next to and both of us immediately got up, gladly abandoned our half-full cups of coffee, and left the restaurant. We returned to the hotel and I found a seat in the training room.

Stephen began to lead us through a process that

was very similar to what we had been through at the Pre-Training Seminar. "Locate your space. . . . Experience how you experience experience. . . ." We located spaces throughout our bodies and were then given a long series of experiences, each introduced by the phrase "Think of a time when . . ." or "Remember when . . . you felt really real . . . you really felt loved . . . you really communicated with someone . . . you were really understood. . . ." As the series ended, Stephen told us to think of the room we were in. He described it in precise detail: "Think of the blue carpet with the gold floral pattern standing out against the background, the three chandeliers, each with brass arms and light bulbs in the shape of candle flames. Now, when you are ready, slowly and gradually open your eyes."

The value of this process for me was, first, a realization of what was really important—that is, those experiences which had been really meaningful in my life. The second realization I had, one which I could not have predicted and would have denied had it been suggested to me, was how few I could remember.

It was after 3 A.M. when I arrived home. My doorman was asleep.

4

Make Your Headache Disappear

TUESDAY NIGHT'S TRAINING was held at the Statler Hilton. It was farther downtown and the hotel lobby seemed busier and more alive, but once I entered the room it could have been the same as the others. The chairs were arranged in the same way, and after I had taken my seat I was aware only of being hemmed in by other people and of feeling good that I had taken a seat near the center where I had an unobstructed view of the dais on which the trainer stood.

I had begun to recognize people by now and had said hello to a few familiar faces on my way into the room. It was reassuring to find in the group people who looked something like my image of myself: young academic types who could have been my neighbors on the Upper West Side of Manhattan or classmates from graduate school. I had also by now begun to have a sense of who some of the other people were, from comments they made to the group as a whole or from conversations shared or overheard during breaks or while waiting to get into the training room at the beginning of a session. There seemed to be a large number of performing artists—actors, singers, and dancers—and a sizable group of mental-health professionals of various persuasions, the most vocal of which seemed to be in the "hipper" rather than the more orthodox sects of psychotherapy. There was at least one self-identified primal therapist, but I hadn't yet met a straight psychoanalyst. Another large group in the audience were in various professions prominent in the New York world—stockbrokers, lawyers, doctors, dentists, optometrists, and the like. A friend of mine who had gone through the training about a year before had mentioned that there was a United States senator in his group, but I never heard of any celebrities in mine.

The Tuesday session got under way with the same abrupt entrance by Guido and then the arrival of Stephen, the trainer. Members of the audience were invited to share with the group. I was surprised at the number of hands that waved in the air in response to the invitation. This was the beginning of a long series of testimonials I would come to associate most clearly with the est training. One young woman spoke tearfully about her husband, who hadn't wanted her to take the est training. Last night when she had gotten home, she found a note from him saying that he had had enough and was leaving. "Thank you," said Stephen. The audience applauded. Several people had comments to make about how they had experienced their day at work after getting much less sleep than usual the night before. All of them seemed to feel they had gotten along just fine. One man claimed that he had always known that he *needed* nine hours of sleep a night; last night he had had only five and he never even noticed it during the day. A middle-aged woman reported that she had had the energy to clean her house for the first time in months. Someone else had finally made a dental appointment she had been putting off too long.

A few of the comments were antagonistic. One man had decided not to come back. He had called the est office to report his decision and to insist that his money be returned. He was transferred around to several people and finally reached one of the trainers (not ours). The trainer he spoke to had said he couldn't have his money back, and if he didn't return to the training, that was the definitive proof that he was an asshole. He came back and told the tale. There was lots of applause. A motherly type announced she was going on a diet, and I heard the sound of 500 hands clapping.

Stephen repeated the main est instruction: Keep your "sole" in the room (he said as he pointed to the bottom of his shoe), follow instructions, and take what you get. He outlined some common pitfalls. One was comparing your experience to that of others.

Take what *you* get was of particular relevance here. Another pitfall was comparing an experience at a certain point in the training to one that was experienced earlier. We were told that *whatever* we were feeling would change. The est training was compared to a roller coaster. If we were down now, we'd eventually be on the way up. If we were up, soon we'd be swooping down a precipice that was described so vividly I felt as though I wanted to hold onto the sides of my seat. Whatever we were experiencing, whatever *was* true for us, then that was what was true for us. Stephen revealed that rocks are hard and water is wet and that's the way it is.

A substantial part of the Tuesday training was devoted to the pronunciation and elaboration of Three Principles.

The First Principle was: "You are perfect *and* there are barriers to the experience of and the expression of that perfection." My interpretation of this was that everyone has more potential than he or she is using and that various forces—neurotic inhibitions, habits, self-defeating attitudes—stand in the way of self-actualization.

The Second Principle stated: "Change causes persistence." I understood this one to mean that as long as you are struggling against something, you are locked into it and perpetuate its influence in your life. The clearest example I could think of was the way in which some couples manage to maintain their relationship by continually struggling with each other. She tries to change him into her image of what he ought to be. The more she tries, the harder he resists and the more intensely they are involved with each other. As a therapist I had seen this phenomenon frequently. I had also noted among my friends how often couples who were breaking up perpetuated their struggles through long divorce fights, with extensive arguments over property division, child custody, and visitation arrangements. Many of these struggles seemed petty and as though they *had* to be masking some purpose other than what was, on the surface, at issue. In such cases, I had often been convinced that the real purpose of the struggle was solely to perpetuate the relationship. If you're fighting with someone, at least you know they *care* about what you're doing and saying. So "change causes persistence" meant that struggling against something perpetuates your involvement in it.

Wow!

We also learned here that there is no such thing as trying. This was demonstrated with a volunteer from the audience who joined the trainer on the stage. "All right, now, Don, let me see you *try* to pick up this chair. See, you *can't try* to pick it up. You either *pick up* the chair or you *don't* pick up the chair. There's no such thing as *trying.*" I was intrigued with this one. When I had, infrequently, made suggestions to patients about things they could actually *do* to change their lives in the way they had been saying

they would like to see things change, I had often
been answered with the comment, "Well, I'll try."
I had come to recognize this phrase as a therapeutic three-strikes-and-you're-out. "I'll try," inevitably
meant, "I won't do it now."

The Third Principle was: "Re-creation causes
disappearance." This was also something I could relate
to my therapeutic experience. I had often encouraged
patients to "get in touch with" feelings that they
seemed to be struggling against and rejecting in themselves, usually because they seemed to think the feelings were unacceptable in some way—harmful, shame-
ful, dangerous, or simply not nice. I had sometimes
tried to compare this to the process of immunization
in medicine: If you receive an inoculation of a small
amount of a mild virus, it can protect you against
coming down with a severe case of the disease. Patients could generally understand the principle of flu
shots, but it was never quite as clear how allowing
yourself to experience, in a therapeutic setting, a small
amount of a dangerous feeling could "immunize" you
against the more powerful feeling that later could
overwhelm your defenses and take hold of your life.

The trainer was illustrating this principle with
several demonstrations, using volunteers, and with exercises the group as a whole participated in. I wasn't
very tuned in to this part. The demonstrations
seemed to consist of tossing a Kleenex box back and

forth from one person to another; then a volunteer stood onstage and clapped two blackboard erasers together. I didn't get it in these concrete forms, but the abstract principle was indeed one that had meaning in my own experience. You re-create (in imagination or fantasy, not necessarily in the reality of the world you live in) disturbing sensations, feelings, or thoughts in order to free yourself from their influence.

The next part of the training seemed to engage the interest of most of the audience; people seemed suddenly to come awake. Everyone was sitting up straighter, and alert listeners were asking questions. We were being taught techniques for accomplishing things in life.

The first was a technique for waking up without an alarm clock, at a specified time, feeling fresh and alive. The technique began in the same manner as had the processes we had done so far. We located our space and then went through the body, locating spaces from our toes to our scalps, putting our consciousness and awareness into each one. Then we went to our beach scene. "Next you visualize a clock, whatever kind you see is all right. . . . No, Robert, it doesn't matter if the one you see is digital, but the one you really have has a dial with hands. Reach out in front of you and set the hands of the clock at the hour you would like to wake up." (If it's a digital model, presumably you

would be allowed to turn the dial until the right numbers appeared). "Then tell yourself that you want
to wake up, say, at 8 A.M., and that you want to
awaken feeling fresh and alive."

That was all there was to it. I was curious about
this technique. It had certainly been my experience
that I sometimes woke up at the time I wanted to,
perhaps a minute or so before the alarm rang. This
usually happened when I was not getting up at my
regular time but had to arise at a specific hour, usually
for something special although not necessarily pleas-
ant. I had also observed that when my schedule for
the next day included an unusually early start it was
almost always because I had to get to an appointment
that was particularly important in some way and about
which I usually had some anxiety.

The second technique was for remembering and
understanding our dreams. The beginning for all techniques was the same: "Locate your space." You then
asked yourself if you wanted to remember and understand your dreams. If your answer was affirmative,
you gave yourself instructions by stating your inten-
tion to do so. This technique was less intriguing to me,
simply because I was aware of how effortlessly people
begin to remember dreams when they enter psychotherapy, if they are working with a therapist who
expresses interest in dream material. Some people beginning psychoanalysis go to a lot of trouble to make

sure they don't lose dream content. Some of them keep a note pad beside their bed, or even a tape recorder, and force themselves awake after each dream period to make notes. Since the stage of sleep in which we dream also happens to be a stage of "light" sleep when we are actually very close to a waking state, it's generally not too difficult to do this.

A third technique, for falling asleep, involved continually locating spaces throughout your body and then repeating the *Relaaaaaaaaaax* instruction three times. You were to continue to locate spaces until you fell deeply asleep.

An interesting technique which est had in common with a variety of other therapies and self-control procedures was the technique for treating a headache, tiredness, or minor aches and pains. All of us in the audience who were experiencing any of these were invited to join in as the trainer led a volunteer onstage through these paces: "Close your eyes and locate your space. Now describe your headache [tiredness, tennis elbow, back pain, et cetera]. Describe it exactly. Note the type of sensation. Is it burning? Is it pressure? Is it sharp and stabbing? Dull and throbbing? Describe the exact location without reference to abstractions. Is it on the left side of your chest, about halfway down between your neck and your waist? Is it moving at all or does it stay in one place? Place your consciousness and awareness into the burning; experience the pressure. Ask yourself where your headache or discomfort would be now on a scale from one to ten, if ten is where you were when you started out. Go through the description again, noting everything about your sensations exactly. Continue until the sensation disappears or is reduced to an acceptable level."

The final technique was a variant of this one. The demonstration in this case was specifically for headaches. Someone who had a headache at the moment was invited to sit on a stool on the stage, while the trainer asked her a series of questions, beginning with the usual instructions for closing eyes and locating your space. The trainer asked her: "If your headache had a geometric shape, what shape would it be?" It was a circle. "If it had a color, what color would it be?" It was bright red. "If your headache were a container that could hold a volume of water, what volume of water would it hold?" This continued for a while; her headache went from round to square to triangular, back to round, to rectangular, to oval. It was red, then blue, orange, and a deep purple, finally fading to a pastel pink. It held a gallon of water, then a quart, a pint, a cup, and on down to just a teaspoon or so. By the time it was a light pink oval holding only a teaspoonful, it had disappeared.

The audience was awestruck. I felt as though I had stumbled into an Oral Roberts revival. Was this a tent pitched on an Arkansas field or a hotel ballroom

in midtown Manhattan? The trainer, seemingly bask-
ing in the unspoken adulation streaming from the audience, expansively invited all the "professionals" in the
group to apply the est techniques in their own professions in any manner that was ethically appropriate. He
stated that est was interested in contributing in whatever way it could to related fields and that those who
were credentialed by the agreements of society to
practice particular professions were encouraged to
take whatever they found valuable in the est training
and apply it to their work. It was at this point that I
decided the appropriate application for a college pro-
fessor to make would be to write a book.

We were given an assignment for the next day.
The first part was to practice one or more of the
techniques. The second part was to think of an "item,"
which was defined as a recurring pattern in your life
that you would like to be rid of.

The evening ended with another process (I had
begun to look forward to these): "Locate your
space." By the time the trainer's voice was saying re-
laaaaax, I had gotten over my annoyance at the faith
healing and was ready to enjoy some simple medita-
tion.

When I arrived home it was again after 3 A.M., so
it seemed appropriate that the technique I should
practice was the one for falling asleep. I had standards
by which to evaluate it. I was scheduled to lecture the

next morning, and if I didn't fall asleep *immediately* I was sure I'd be a somnambulist in class. *Relaaaaa- aaaaaax*, I droned to myself within a microsecond of my head's making contact with the pillow. My con- sciousness and awareness were next engaged when I opened my eyes at eight thirty, just before the alarm rang.

I got through my lecture with ease. After class a student asked me to give him a few days' extension on the deadline for his term paper. I agreed but stated firmly that I would have to receive it by a certain date. "I'll try," said the student. I smiled and didn't say anything.

5

What's <u>Your</u> Item?

THE WEDNESDAY NIGHT TRAINING, like the one preceding it, opened with a session of "sharing." Anyone
who "shared" received the trainer's direct attention,
and I guessed that the person speaking felt as though he
or she were having a private conversation. There were
a few sharers, however, who played to the crowd.
Everyone was applauded by the group, but clearly
some were winning more applause than others. It was
sort of a psychological version of Ted Mack's Ama-
teur Hour. The trainer picked up on the dynamic occurring here and reminded us that clapping indicated
simply an acknowledgment; it was not a vote. The
purpose of sharing was constantly reinforced: "If you
keep something inside of you, it runs your life." Some
people, mainly the chronic complainers, were put
down rather sharply by Stephen: "Dora, your *whole
life* is about having a headache. You are run by your
headaches. Take a look at that."

I was never moved to share. But if I had, my story would have run something like this: During the training I have been bored, amused, irritated, angry, insulted, and interested, and I have been excited when something that was said seemed to connect with my life, usually when an est phrase or concept plugged into some bit of what I considered to be fundamental wisdom. Outside the training, from the appetizer of the Pre-Training Seminar through those first two evenings of the training itself, I have been as high as a supersonic transport at cruising altitude.

I had indeed been bouncing through my workaday life with the enthusiasm and élan I normally felt only episodically, at those times when things were going specially well. I felt great. Nothing had changed in my outside world: New York City was still going bankrupt, the noise on Broadway just outside my windows was as loud as ever, I was not in a particularly stimulating period of my work. I had not just won a lottery—but damn! I felt as if I had.

The quality of my casual interactions with people had seemed to change. Taxi drivers spontaneously offered to wait and watch me go inside my door at night. I walked through a subway station, and as I passed two boys who looked like college students, one said to the other, "Now *there's* a pretty girl." Walking out of a store in my neighborhood I had stumbled and tripped on the door sill, and a man

standing on the sidewalk nearby told me to enjoy my
"trip." I laughed and thanked him for the send-off. I
guessed that somehow I must have been exuding the
exhilaration I felt. But I wasn't eager to state this publicly in the form of a testimonial for est, since I had
determined to suspend my critical faculties while I
was experiencing the training.

After Stephen declared the sharing to be over, he
told us we would begin the setup for what he called
the Truth Process. This was to take hours. And hours.
It began with an explanation of a pie diagram Stephen
chalked onto the blackboard. The whole pie was labeled the "condition," and one wedge of it was an
"item." One retrieved an item from a condition by
means of a "hook." Well, all right, I thought, if that's
what they want to call things I guess I can stand it,
but I still don't know what "condition" or "hook"
means. At least "item" had been defined for us the
night before; as homework we were told to choose an
"item"—a persistent pattern in our life we wished to
eliminate.

Stephen asked for a volunteer from the audience
who was willing to share his or her item with the
group as a demonstration. There must have been
seventy-five hands in the air, all confirming my belief that middle-class Americans have no sense of
privacy. I have never ever understood why people
like houses with open front lawns running down to the

street. I hate grass. If I *had* to have a front yard I'd dig up the lawn, pave it over with bricks, and build a wall as close to the street as building-setback regulations would allow. There wasn't a chance that I would share *my* item with the group.

The first person called on was a man I had noticed at an earlier stage of the training. He was one of four or five people that I had guessed had fairly serious psychological problems, judging by things they said in earlier periods of sharing. I wished the trainer hadn't picked him to go first. He began in a roundabout way with a loosely connected stream of ideas for which the listener had to supply the connecting threads. It wasn't totally incoherent, but he became more tangential the more he talked. If he had been my patient I would have gently but firmly stopped him from going further, said something intended to provide a connection to external reality, and consulted with the head of the clinic about additional measures.

Stephen seemed to have no such concern. "Dennis," he yelled at him, "*cut out the soap opera!* You're just running your tape. You're not sharing your experience, you're *dramatizing* it. Now I want you to tell me the *truth* about it."

I was shocked. I couldn't decide whether I thought Dennis was being exploited or respected as a human being who, despite obvious weaknesses, was capable of strength. I continued to struggle with this uncertainty as I listened. Dennis's item had something to do with an unsettling sexual situation in which he had not been able to perform to his satisfaction. Stephen urged him, through a series of progressively more specific questions, to clarify his feelings and tell it like it was. The process was similar to the est headache cure and demonstrated the operation of Observation, which had been the first step above the line on the Scale of Knowing. Dennis was announced to have "gotten his item" when he had pared away all the excess and was able to state his concern as a bare matter of fact. His item was "a stuck-ness in his cock."

Other people were called on. By this time the ranks of potential volunteers had grown considerably. Undoubtedly I was getting some perverse voyeuristic gratifications out of observing all this, but I was still not moved to the exhibitionism that seemed to be infecting the rest of the group. A girl spoke next of her constant feeling of failure related to the rejection she always felt from her brother. Somehow, in a way I rather marveled at, the trainer was able to convey to her that her brother was doing whatever he was doing in relation to love. She was making her brother wrong, a defensive tactic we all employed in our struggles to maintain our own "Righteousness." We were told that we'd rather be right than alive. And so we were: dead right. We maintained our Righteousness in such ways as proving ourselves to be failures. We were asked to think about who would be proved wrong if our lives were to work. The answer was . . . *you.*

An older woman spoke through tears. Crying, she confessed that this was the first occasion on which she had admitted to herself that she felt guilty over not having helped her father enough when he needed it. She had acted out of her own Righteousness. She stated that she also blamed her mother for not having been a good enough wife to her father. "Notice what you *get* out of doing your usual number," the trainer said. "You get to be right. And *that's all you get. You don't get your life to work.*"

An attractive black woman indicated that her item had to do with her pattern of rejecting men. The trainer was unable to pin her down to the specifics required for an item to be acceptable. She was accused of doing her number, running her tape, reading her script. I began to notice the similarity to a lot of concepts from Transactional Analysis.

Hands continued to wave in the air each time someone finished going through their item with Stephen. It was an endless process. I thought that most people by now had a perfectly good idea of what an acceptable item was; the general principles had been demonstrated several times. But it no longer seemed as though people were volunteering in order to get some clarification of vaguely articulated distress. The ones who kept raising their hands at this point seemed to want the limelight or the attention of Stephen's concentration on the troubles in their life.

This was the part of the est training which I felt to be the most unbearable. I thought that if I heard one more person say, "*My* item is . . . ," I'd scream. It was damnably frustrating. Apparently even the trainer felt this. When the same question had been raised for approximately the tenth time, Stephen exploded. "*All right, you people*. We'll stay here *all night* if that's what it takes for you to *get* this. *Guido*, tell the hotel we're taking this room straight through tomorrow. I can stay here longer than you can."

It was clear that there was no way we were going to be allowed a break until people started *getting* it. For the first time I began to experience the physical discomfort of the training. My back ached, my head hurt, my eyelids were heavy weights. I simply could not endure being there. At this point I tuned out of the next few hours of work on people's items and decided to spend the time Observing: my tiredness, my aches and pains, my pangs of hunger, my thirst, my desire to go to the bathroom, my craving for a cigarette.

When my consciousness came back to what was going on in the training, Stephen was talking about Problems. We were told that "solving" problems just creates further problems. If we were realistic about such things, we would realize that we could not exist

without problems. Problems were simply the next
thing to be handled in life. Even if your whole life was
as nice as a vacation at the beach, you'd still have
problems: You'd have to find food to eat and water to
drink and a way to get out of the sun when you had
had enough. The trouble with problems in our lives
was simply the way we experienced them. We told
lies about them. For example, we'd say, "I'd like to go
to the movies, but I have work to do." Nonsense, said
Stephen. The "but" is a lie because "but" negates
everything that comes before it. If we really wanted
to go to the movies, we would go to the movies. Stating it the way we do, however, allows us to have a
problem. What we get out of that is the rightness of
our lives' not working. To avoid lying, one could sub-
stitute "and" for "but": "I want to go to the movies
and I have work to do."

The thing to do with problems was to give them
away. An anecdote was recounted of one of the est
trainers at an airport, wanting to send two bags to two
different cities and being told that this was somehow
impossible according to airline policy. "Don't make
the other person wrong" was the first step. Acknowledge that you've gotten their message. "Yes, I understand that what I want to do is impossible *and* I wonder
if you could tell me how you'd do it if you were in
my position." The value of giving away problems was
not only recommended for travelers struggling with
the logistics of the transportation industry, it was also

recommended that management give problems to the organization's employees. Stephen said that when this had been tried a feeling of participation and creativity occurred and the whole organization rose like a rocket.

Stephen began another lecture. It was a presentation of information, or what estians persisted in calling data, pronounced "datta." This was titled the Anatomy of Experience. Anatomy seemed to mean components or constituent parts. Eventually, Stephen told us, when we finally got to the point of doing the much-heralded Truth Process, we would be associating each of these components of experience with our items.

The first part of the anatomy of experience was bodily sensations, including their location. These were to be described exactly and in detail. Next were emotions or feelings, such as anger, joy, or fear. Third were attitudes, points of view, and states of mind, including such global generalizations as "I am a failure." Fourth were behaviors, facial expressions, and body postures. Fifth were "considerations," statements generally prefaced by "I think" that were somewhat more limited in scope than attitudes. Considerations also seemed to include beliefs and evaluative statements, as in "Nice girls don't." Sixth and last on the list were images from the past.

The Truth Process was going to be done lying down. They had worked out a system for stacking the chairs to get them out of the way. It was at times like this that I was totally impressed by the est organization. Within what could not have been more than a few minutes, all two hundred fifty of us had, in orderly rows, stacked our chairs in designated out-of-the-way places along the walls of the room, no more than five chairs to a stack. Somehow there was room for everyone to find a place to stretch out on the carpet.

This was the first process we had done lying down. I was curious as to what difference it might make. It seemed, afterward, that it was even easier to "get into the experience" than it had been when I was sitting up. I wondered if lying down in this way tended to promote and encourage regression, in the way that the couch in psychoanalysis was presumed to function.

"Locate your space. . . ." The usual set of instructions followed as we located spaces throughout our bodies in very, very great detail. Then we were sent to the beach, where we were to create our items. The guided fantasy to the visual imagery of the seaside was embellished with the aid of a tape recording of surf sounds. We were instructed to participate in the process only as long as we were still experiencing our items. As soon as we had "experienced them out," we were to turn over onto our stomachs and go back to the beach until the trainer told us to return to the hotel room. "Now put your consciousness and awareness into whatever bodily sensations come up for you. Notice the nature of the sensation and its location. Associate the sensation with your item. Keep associating your body sensations with your item. Take whatever comes up for you. Now, notice your emotions. Describe these emotions. Observe them. Associate these feelings with your item."

And so it went through the list. I felt as though I had "completed" associating components of experience with my own private item about halfway through this process. I turned over and went to my beach, which happened to be on the Outer Banks of North Carolina: Ocracoke Island, to be exact. But how could they keep me down on Ocracoke once I began to hear what was going on in the Statler Hilton ballroom? Volunteers were distributing vomit bags to trainees in distress throughout the room. People were crying, moaning, sobbing. *"You son of a bitch!"* yelled someone near me. *"Fuck you!"* rang out from several places in the room. A scream pierced the profanity. *"Noooooooooooooo"* came from someone I was sure must be dying. The anguish of pain—past or present—was everywhere in that room.

I thought of how desperate people had seemed while going through their items at the outset of the evening and wondered about the wisdom, from a psychiatric point of view, of encouraging people to experience the most painful parts of their lives in a setting of group contagion.

Despite my "considerations," everyone seemed to be there and to look at least superficially all right when the process was over and we were instructed to come back from our beaches and bring our consciousness and awareness into the room. The session ended in a normal fashion with everyone trouping out to the coat racks in the lobby, getting their things together, and finding rides home or companions for their journeys.

I was high again the next day. The only downs I had were in the training room itself, when I thought it was boring or tedious or when I was noticing how many hours I had been sitting, without moving, on a straight-backed chair. From the time I left the training, again about 3 A.M., until I returned the next evening I felt uniformly good. I had the suspicion I was walking around with a smile on my face.

6

Get Off Your Act!

FOR THE THURSDAY NIGHT SESSION the room was arranged differently. There was a long platform extending across the front of the room, like a fashion show runway. Chairs were not grouped into sections but stretched in straight rows from one side of the room to the other. When I came through the door I was immediately sent to a seat in the first row. I had the impression that things had suddenly become more serious, as though the preceding evenings had been something of a warm-up and now we were about to get to the bottom line.

At 7 P.M. Guido marched onto the platform and waited a few seconds for the group to stop talking and get themselves arranged at attention. People were responding to cues much more quickly now. We were actually a well-trained audience. Guido announced that there would be no further talking in the room for the rest of the session. There would be no sharing tonight. The process was scheduled to take the entire evening.

We sat quietly, with hands in lap, for many minutes. Occasionally my concentration would be interrupted by the sound of someone opening the door. Finally Stephen arrived and began to give us the instructions for the process. We would be going up to the front of the room, in groups, and taking designated places on the platform facing the rest of the trainees. We were to stand there, "being with" the others and experiencing whatever came up for us. "Follow instructions and take what you get." We were told to take a look at the barriers that arose. The things that would come up for us in this exercise would be the same things that kept our relationships with people from working in our lives.

I was excited that the front row was going up to the platform first. We were told to get up from our seats and file across the front of the room. Our places on the platform were marked with masking tape. When we were all in proper position on the platform, we were told to stand there with our hands at our sides, "being with" the others in the room.

"Make contact with people all over the room. Don't just concentrate on people near the front. *Get off your act!* I *know* how together you are; what I want to see is how afraid you are. Notice the numbers you do to keep yourself from being with people . . .

whatever your act is: being tough . . . or cool . . . or sexy . . . or hip . . . or intellectual . . . or going unconscious. *Get in touch with your experience of whatever it is that you're afraid of, whatever your act is hiding.*"

At an almost imperceptible signal which on repetition throughout the evening began to sound like two exhalations into the microphone of the public-address system, a group of est graduates who had been sitting and standing in a formal portrait arrangement in the back of the room began to move forward. As they reached the platform and stepped up on it, the noise of their feet sounded like the boots of an army. Some of them went in back of the platform and stood behind us. I didn't know what they were doing. Others, maybe six or seven, walked down the platform and then suddenly turned on their heels and faced someone. No one was standing in front of me, but I could see out of the corners of my eyes that they were standing very near. I had a hard time reconciling those promises of postgraduate aliveness, natural behavior, and spontaneity with the catatonic stares and rigid posturings of the estian troops.

Stephen's cadence continued. He walked back and forth in front of the platform. "Get *off* it, Bob! Stop resisting. . . . Let it come up. Get in touch with your fear. Be conscious of your experience. GET OFF YOUR ACT! Sandy, don't go unconscious, *be* with people. I *know* how tough you are, what I want to see is what you're AFRAID of." Occasionally Guido would yell from the back of the room, "GET OFF IT!"

It wasn't long before people standing on the platform were crying. We had to keep looking straight ahead out into the two hundred faces remaining in the audience, so I could not see people standing with me on the platform; I *could* hear them, though, and I was amazed. Men and women were crying, some sobbing, some choking, some just whimpering. I wasn't crying. I didn't feel fear. Stephen walked by and paused as he went by me. At the instant he passed I felt that I had lost most of the conscious control I possessed. My face was tingling, burning, feeling as though a cold wind were blowing from the west. I could feel my muscles moving spasmodically—a tic in my cheek, a twitch of my shoulder, a tremor in my left leg. During the entire process I was alternately bored, sad, embarrassed, and amused. But the major thing I kept "getting" was sadness. That was definitely coming up for me.

Next to me in the lineup was a woman who seemed to be about sixty years old. She looked and spoke as though she were an actress, although I can't specify what it was about her that suggested that to me. As Stephen passed in front of her screaming "LET ME SEE YOUR FEAR!" she began singing out loud.

The words of "God Bless America" filled the room. It was shocking. Stephen stood with his nose less than an inch from hers and ordered her to get off her act. She kept singing for longer than I would have been able to. I was stunned by her performance. My first association was that she was whistling in the dark. Stephen attacked her relentlessly, scornfully calling her on her act, her number, her tape, her game. I knew that in some so-called therapeutic circles this kind of attack, euphemized into a "confrontation," was thought to be useful and ultimately helpful for the person being confronted. Even if it were so, I didn't think these bullying tactics could be justified. I thought Stephen was in fact probably right about what this woman was doing. Her behavior was in the service of resistance. Then I flashed on that scene from the film *Casablanca* in which all the French people in Rick's Café respond to the German soldiers' songs by drowning them out with an enthusiastic rendering of the "Marseillaise." I had always loved that scene. I was proud of that woman singing next to me. God bless America. Indeed, I hoped so.

One of the est volunteers stood in front of me, her toes almost touching mine and her face no more than a few inches away. I still wasn't frightened. In fact, this was a relief. I enjoyed changing the focus of my eyes away from that large sea of faraway faces. I had been noticing that it seemed easier for me to "be with" people than for people to "be with" me. Scanning the audience, I had been surprised how often someone's eyes would skitter sidewise just as they made contact with mine. But the goon-squad member in front of me had no difficulty with eye contact. She stared hard, compellingly. She stood there for a shorter time than I had seen her standing in front of other people, and then she turned and walked away. At another signal that breathed through the public-address system, all the est volunteers left the platform and returned to formation at the back of the room.

Stephen told us we would be going back to our seats and were to sit for the rest of the time with our arms and legs uncrossed, being with the people who would follow us on the platform. "Don't go back into yourselves. Don't go into your space. *Be with them.*" When we got the word, the person at the end of the platform turned, then the next and the next and the next, and we all filed off and back to our front-row seats. The next row was already filing onto the platform.

The procedure was continued until all 250 people had been on the platform. About forty people at a time would be standing in front, stretched across the room. I could see now that the est volunteers in back of the platform were there to catch people who fell, although nobody did. Whenever someone began to sway or appear a little weak in the knees, the person in back covering that section of the platform would seem to get prepared for a rescue catch. In each group, four or five people would eventually be crying. The rest just stood there, for the most part looking intimidated and, even worse, as though they would do *anything* to please the trainer and avoid his wrath. Occasionally someone would begin to laugh, but Stephen never let that go unnoticed. He would shout that person's name and remind him or her of unexperienced fear.

"Do you want to know why there's no love in the world? LOOK AT THAT, LOOK AT THOSE FACES! That's why none of your relationships work, why you can't BE WITH people!"

Everyone had been to the front of the room. Now we were told how to stack our chairs to clear the room so we could lie on the floor. Two hundred and fifty people stacked their chairs out of the way and found their places on the carpet. It occurred to me that the mood in the room might not be all that different from the mood among people who were resignedly lining up to be shot. There were no trenches here, however. Stephen reminded us that the training room had been created as a "safe space." He repeated information he had given us near the beginning of the training (which had seemed to me then to have been so irrelevant that I hadn't bothered to remember it): There were "specially trained" est volun-

teers stationed outside the doors of the room, to make
sure that no unauthorized person could enter. They
were in charge of "keeping the lions away." I later
heard from a friend who had on several occasions performed this function during his period of est volunteering that the people outside the doors were
"psyched up" to an incredible frame of mind where
they would literally have *died* before letting anyone
through those doors. They were soldiers for est.

So there we were, on the carpet. And not a lion
in sight. "Create your space. Find a space in your left
foot. Good. Find a space in your right foot. Thank
you. Find a space in your ankles . . . in your lower leg
. . . in your knees . . find a space in your knee joints
. . . in your thighs . . . in your hip joints. Good. Find
a space between your genitals and your rectum and
come up into your torso, through your pelvic bone in
the front. Come up through your left side and your
right side. Come up through your buttocks to the base
of your spine in the back. Fine. Come up through your
small intestine, your large intestine. Good. Find a
space in your abdomen. . . . Come up through your
stomach, your digestive organs. Good. Find your liver
on the right side . . . your pancreas . . . your spleen.
Fine. Thank you. Come up through your diaphragm
muscles into your chest cavity. . . . Find a space in
your lungs. . . . Experience your breathing. Find a
space in your heart. Find a space in your shoulders . . .
in your back . . . in the muscles that stretch across at

the top of your back. Good. Find a space in your neck . . . in the back of your head . . . in your cheeks . . . in your nasal passages . . . in your eyes . . . in your forehead . . . in your brain . . . at the top of your skull.

"Now take a deep breath and as you let it out, *relaaaaaaaaaaaaaaaax.* Take another deep breath and as you let it out, *relaaaaaaaaaaaaaaaax.* Take a deep breath and this time as you let it out, *relaaaaaaaaaaaaaaaaaaax.* Let go of your legs. Good. Let go of your arms. Good. Let go of any tightness in your body. Let go of the tight places. Fine. Thank you.

"Expand your space to include the person lying next to you. You are afraid of this person, terrified of this person. Experience your fear. Now expand your space to include the people on both sides of you. You are very frightened of both these people. Experience your fear, your terror. Get in touch with it. Good. Expand your space to include three people around you. You are terrified. . . . More frightened than you have ever been of anything. Experience your fear. Fine. Expand your space to include ten people around you. Get in touch with being frightened. They are all around you. . . . *There's nowhere for you to turn. . . . No place to escape!* You are terrified. Expand your space to include everybody in this room. . . . You are *afraid* of *every single person* in this room. Focus on your experience of fear."

All this took a very long time to say. At each new

suggestion, fortissimo screams swelled out of the crowd. I thought I might as well join them to see what it felt like. It was OK, but I didn't experience any cathartic relief. Maybe that was because I didn't have any feelings I had not been able to discharge in other ways. Maybe it was because I was too well defended. Maybe it was because I was too busy giggling about what this must have sounded like to the people at the black-tie dinner taking place in the room next door.

The instructions continued. There was an imagery exercise where we were told to imagine ourselves in the following situation: "You are driving alone in your car at night along a dark city street. Your car stops suddenly and you can't get it started again. You sit there alone in the dark, turning the key and pressing the accelerator down. But nothing happens. You'll have to leave your car. You are not far from home. You get out of the car and start to walk down the street. Before you reach the corner you hear footsteps behind you. The footsteps get louder and faster and you realize that someone is after you. You pick up speed and turn the corner toward your building. You're going as fast as you can and the footsteps are gaining on you. You run into your building. The elevator comes quickly and you reach your floor. You're hurrying to the door of your apartment and fumbling for your keys. You open the door and slam it quickly behind you, pushing the bolt of the deadlock firmly into place. As the door locks you breathe a sigh of relief that you are finally safe. You turn around to walk into your bedroom *and you are facing two big men!*"

The training room was by now Pandemonium, the capital of hell. The screams were what Orwell called "bellyfeel." It blew me away.

We were warned that there was a joke in store. The punch line was that everybody else was afraid of *us*. There were some gratuitous insults thrown to the psychiatric community, with a joke ending, "Guess what? Your *shrink* is afraid of *you*."

"Everyone is afraid of everyone else. Why do you think men need to go around with all those muscles? Why do women have to carry around all that equipment for fixing their faces and their hair?" Everyone in the room seemed to be giggling. The laughter crescendoed to the guffaw level. We were encouraged to use our new knowledge to experience and observe everyone else being afraid of us out there in the world of reality. "I want you to *give* the ulcers this week, not *get* them. Your state of mind should be such that when *you* walk down the street this week, people cross to the other side."

We were now halfway through the training, although our trainer insisted that we had at this point gotten merely fifteen percent of it. I couldn't find the members of my carpool in the lobby, so I walked out onto Seventh Avenue alone. A clock said three thirty. In the morning. I crossed over to the taxi stand in front of Madison Square Garden and waited for a cab. There weren't any other members of the training on the street. I couldn't understand why they all went out exits on the other sides of the hotel. This was only an observation. I was standing on a dark Manhattan street in the middle of the night by myself. I was not afraid. To be as honest as possible about it, I think I was probably looking for a fight.

I went to a party that Saturday night. I remembered as I walked in the door that I was still within the confines of my "agreements." This was probably the first time I had been to a party since the age of sixteen or so without having some kind of consciousness-altering liquid or other substance. I would have enjoyed some wine, but I knew it was the taste I was wanting, not the effects. I stuck to ginger ale and had a wonderful time. I don't mean to suggest that such events took on cosmic proportions in my life. If I had been looking for the "miracles" that some of the est graduates I had spoken with had claimed were the results of their training, I would have been disappointed. One of my virtues has always been to find pleasure in small things. One of the small things that was contributing to my mid-est high was the realization that I had gotten through what were for me many unusual deprivations without major discomfort. I had never doubted that I could *endure* deprivation, but what was of interest now was that I had gone without eating, sleeping, smoking, drinking, talking, or walking at whim. It was very interesting to know that none of these things were a "big deal" in my life. It approached the narcissistic invulnerability of feeling that I had no needs. I *was* arrogant during this period between the two parts of the training, but it was a quiet arrogance. Mainly I felt very much in charge of my life. And powerful.

7

Orange Liquid Drips

THE MID-TRAINING SEMINAR, described as a bridge between the two parts, was held the following Tuesday evening. It began with testimonials, introduced as an opportunity for us all to share the "movement" that had taken place in our lives. Hands were waving in the crowded air. Margaret was called on first. She had suffered continuous back pain from crushed vertebrae for years. She had now been completely free of the pain for five days. (Faith healing was not likely to impress me.) Dorothy was next and identified herself as a compulsive eater. She told of picking up a guy over the weekend and using est's encouragement of self-expression as an excuse for behavior she herself found degrading. Then she dumped him, went home, and overate. She realized that she used eating to keep her out of potential relationships.

Molly had not seen her lover for four months.

They got together over the weekend to talk and didn't stop for eighteen hours. Rosalind reported a history of going through relationship after relationship looking for something wrong with each of them. She had been trying to understand this pattern in therapy for a long time now, but it wasn't until her session following last week's training that she suddenly "got" that she was afraid that other men would leave her as her father had when she was young. Grace had always been frightened of heights. She had climbed a ladder yesterday, realized what she was doing, and climbed higher.

Craig, a heavily bearded man, talked disjointedly about his negative self-image and his fear of going crazy. He had "gotten" that it was OK to have revealed himself in the training. Three women, each in turn, stated that they had been suicidal and through the Truth Process had realized that they *did* want to live. Glen talked about Stephen, our trainer. He felt he could have "taken him on" and had a fantasy of upstaging Stephen and his bellowing style. He had also fantasized slipping a knife in between Stephen's ribs. Stephen wouldn't bleed.

Ron had felt he was being run by Stephen. He had continued to hear Stephen's voice over the last five days. He had also told his wife he loved her more in the last three days than in the past twenty years. Gertrude still had a headache which persisted despite her applications of the est headache cures and her attempts at re-creating the headache to make it disappear. Her announcement received notably less applause than the back pain cure. Philip followed with an account of his use of the waking-up technique. He awoke fifteen minutes early feeling great. He fell back to sleep "for five minutes" and awoke four hours later, having dreamed of snorting cocaine and shooting heroin. I remembered a joke I had read somewhere recently about the large segment of the population today for whom opium is the opiate of the masses.

Jean had been dreading to make a particular telephone call. On Sunday she had made the call and had been fully confident of her ability to handle the situation. Henry, a middle-aged man who appeared frustrated, told us that before the Truth Process he had really struggled to get his item. Then he was totally disrupted by the din that broke out in the room. He did not even try to participate in the Fear Process because he knew the noise would happen again. Barbara had used her newly acquired communication abilities to communicate with a man sitting across the aisle from her on a Fifth Avenue bus. He got off at her stop and invited her to join him for lunch in a neighborhood restaurant. Over lunch, she talked of her hopes and plans to get into the field of international banking. It turned out that he had numerous relevant contacts and had already put her in touch with people she was looking forward to talking with.

Howard climaxed the sharing. He began by recalling how idiotic he had thought the question about results had been on the application questionnaire. He had initially written "nothing specific" and then run into trouble from one of the hawk-eyed gatekeepers. He had been furious. "If that's what *I* want from the training, why can't I put it down? Just because *you* wanted to do better on your job or whatever you said doesn't mean that should be *my* goal." The gatekeeper had sent Howard over to the corner of the lobby to "think about it," noting that Howard would not be able to enter the training room until he, the gatekeeper, approved the questionnaire as being appropriately complete. Howard said he was so angry that he decided that he'd put down something so absurd that it couldn't *possibly* come true. That would show them. So he wrote that the specific result he would like to produce from the training was to become rich and famous. A joke, the most ridiculous thing he could think of, his way of making est "wrong." Then, yesterday, he had gone to his office at the usual time and begun the day in a state of reasonable satisfaction with where he was at this time professionally, having begun his own free-lance business about six months ago. He was doing well, especially when you took into consideration the economic situation. In mid-morning he received a telephone call from his former employers, a large corporation, asking him if he could arrange his schedule to meet with them that afternoon. He had laughingly, to himself, thought of this as clearing a space for the meeting.

His former company had run into a problem in the area of his expertise and wanted him to solve it for them. They asked if he'd be willing to give them thirty days of his time in the next six months—at the rate of two thousand dollars a day. He was so excited at this point in telling the story that his words were coming out a little jumbled, but it was clear that he thought "est works" even when he had tried to make it wrong. The leader of the seminar, Mike, knew enough to quit when he was ahead. He ended the sharing.

An est staff member joined the seminar leader on the stage to plug the graduate seminars we would have the "opportunity" to enroll in after completing our training. There were six standard seminars, to be taken in sequence. Each included from ten to twelve meetings, lasting approximately three hours each. I figured out, based on the schedule they outlined, that each seminar lasted about three and a half months. It would take only slightly less than two years to complete the series. There were also various other kinds of est activities. Special graduate events were held periodically. Sometimes shorter seminar series on specific

topics were held. A graduate could also volunteer to
assist in the est office. Graduates could assist at future
trainings. Clearly there was a future for you in est. I
remembered that when I lived in Chicago people used
to joke about Adlerian therapists, who viewed the development of social interest as a prime criterion of
mental health. It was rumored that they encouraged
their patients to join the Hyde Park Co-op, a coopera-
tive grocery store known for its lengthy and frequent
shareholders' meetings, fund-raising events, and charter flights. It seemed as though the opportunities for
"participation" in est were even greater. What a
classy singles' bar.

We did two processes the evening of the Mid-
Training. The first, as we sat on our chairs, began as
usual with systematic relaxation—uncross your arms
and your legs . . . create your space—and proceeded
on to guided fantasy. We were to imagine that our
bodies were made of clear glass. Empty at the outset,
our glass bodies would then be filled with an orange
liquid. We were to imagine that there were valves at
the ends of our toes and our fingers. "The orange liquid
goes down, slowly, slowly. As it goes it takes with it
any tension, holding, soreness, or stress. These things
disappear as the orange liquid disappears, first from the
top of your heads, inch by inch down below your ears
and neck, and on out the valves you have opened on
your fingers and then again through the lower body

and the toe valves." Then we were instructed to go back through our bodies and shake out any drops of orange liquid that remained anywhere. The clear glass containers of our corporeal beings were to be filled with energy, aliveness, fresh mountain air. We breathed in the pine-scented breeze for a few minutes before extending our space to awareness of the room and returned to New York, where the air is rarely satisfactory.

The second process of the evening, for which we stretched out on the floor, had us expanding our awareness to the people next to us, to the whole room we were lying in, out into the lobby, through the doors onto Forty-second Street, east and west across Manhattan, down to the Battery and up to the Bronx, throughout the five boroughs, New York State, New Jersey, all of New England, the whole East Coast, across the continent, around the world, and out to the edge of the universe. The space travel took rather a long time, given its sci-fi orientation. It must have been more than a half hour before we accomplished reentry and woke up on the floor of a hotel near Grand Central.

I had especially liked these last two processes. The whimsy of the orange liquid drip appealed to me, and the journey to the edge of the universe left me in a very expansive mood. (The person next to me had expanded his universe into sleep.) I shared a cab home with a psychiatrist who had found these exercises to be excruciating. He had felt compelled to move around, as lying on the floor felt like torture. I was about to risk a psychodynamic interpretation of his difficulties when he mentioned that he had chronic back problems and his muscles had been in spasm for two days. He looked so uncomfortable, I couldn't bear to suggest that he was the source of his own pain. We talked then about how relieved we both had felt when the leader of the second process had brought us all back, step by step, to the room. I had overheard several people commenting as they left the hotel that night that they had been afraid of being left in space. It's interesting, the different ways we have.

8

What Is Reality?

I DID NOT WAKE UP without an alarm on Saturday. I got out of bed at seven so I would have time to eat a substantial breakfast. Thanks to a brief infatuation with the writings of Adelle Davis a few years ago, I had stocked my refrigerator with steak and cottage cheese. When it came right down to it, though, I settled for coffee and cheddar. On the subway I wondered where all the other people were going at that hour on a weekend.

I was beginning to feel like a resident of the Statler Hilton. I recognized some of my classmates in the elevator and was surprised by how much younger and more vulnerable everyone seemed to look, but before I jumped to any conclusions about the Ponce de Leon effects of the est training, I realized that for the first time I was seeing the members of my group in weekend garb. Every other occasion we had been together had been an evening during the week, and almost everyone had then been coming directly from work. There had been greater variety to people's appearances during the week. Now we were almost all wearing blue denim.

The day began with sharing. We still had Stephen as our trainer, which I understood to be unusual; it was more common to have two different trainers for the two parts of the training. A couple of people shared their admiration of Stephen, which had evidently been brought home for them by the relatively lackluster performance of the Mid-Training Seminar leader. The people who spoke of Stephen's great effect on them seemed to have been caught up mostly in their experience of him as an incredibly attractive powerful force. He was given acknowledgment for never having faltered, never having evaded a question. They had liked his booming voice. One man connected the intensity of his response to Stephen's strength to a realization he reached concerning his own act. He had "gotten" that it was his pose to be gentle and unassuming as a disguise for anger which he might reveal if he behaved powerfully.

It seemed to me that the sharing was definitely not as enthusiastic as it had been before. At this point I was notably struck with the brilliance of the est packaging. Stephen gave us another money-back offer. Even though we had been through fifty percent of the training in terms of time, he re-emphasized that it had only been fifteen percent of the content. If we were dissatisfied, we could leave during the break today and get our tuition returned. All you had to do to arrange this was to drop your name tag in the box by the door as you left for the break. The name tags that were collected would be matched with application forms back at the est headquarters, and tuition refunds would be mailed out as soon as possible. This, of course, had the effect of forcing each of us to make another decision for est, to recommit ourselves to the training. I thought it was like adult baptism.

After we had been given the option of departing—which, as far as I was able to find out, nobody took—we went back to what seemed like the first night of the training all over again. We were still being called assholes. (And I had been feeling so terrific all week!) More specifically, we did not know our ass from a hole in the ground. The analogy was used of reading a manual on driving a car and learning it all accurately, with the single exception that the words "rearview mirror" are switched for the words "steering wheel." Stephen's dramatic talents were admirably displayed as he pantomimed getting into the car, sitting down and buckling up, starting the car, and driving off down the street with our hands firmly on the edges of the rearview mirror. When the car inevitably cracks up, we attribute it to outside forces such as God. This is at the level of mystery, where we experience "reality" as a reflection of whatever agreements we have made with authority. We had to learn to respect Reality, which is "substantial, persistent, and will knock you on your ass."

A long interaction began between Stephen and Gus, a trainee sitting in the front row who volunteered an answer to the question of the manner in which one determines what is reality. Gus's efforts to give an explanation that would be satisfactory to Stephen were protean. The example being used was the reality of the wall in the front of the room. Gus at first tried to claim that he assessed its reality through his senses, then his reason. With each suggestion, Stephen would run through a "but what if you couldn't" do whatever it was Gus was claiming he did. In every instance the wall was still there. Respect for reality means don't walk into walls.

According to Stephen there were two tests for reality. The first was merely an interim test: "reasonableness," or agreement. Agreement could reflect either consensus or authority. It was logical, believed, consistent, natural, normal, fitting and proper, predictable. The second and ultimate test for reality was "physicalness," which included form, dimension, and existence in time. Stephen drew two circles on the blackboard. In one he wrote "unreal" and in the other "real." What is unreal is that which we know by agreement or measurement; we are "at effect" with this. We are "at cause" with that which is real, that which exists in our experience. Those things which exist by agreement are illusion; we believe they're real but they're not. When we recognize that what is really real for us is our own experience, we create the world.

Stephen drew more circles on the blackboard. One circle represented My Experience. Another circle, separate from and not overlapping the first, represented Your Experience. Yet a third autonomous circle was Agreement. Stephen asserted further that the Now is all there is. The Now is not in between past and future. It transcends past and future and thus leads to total responsibility. I didn't understand that, but since I wasn't required to believe it I just took what I got—which during this part of the training wasn't much.

Disagreement was defined as attempts at change or resistance. Disagreement perpetuates the agreement. An example was offered: "There are pink elephants on the ceiling." Denying this acknowledges that you understand what is meant by "pink elephants" and thus asserts their existence. If one said, "There are clebs on the ceiling," there would be no understanding.

I was relieved when Stephen moved on to False Cause. He defined cause as the point where we stop further search. He had six or seven volunteers from the audience come up to the stage and stand single file, in a row. He pushed into the first person, who pushed into the second person, who pushed into—and so on down the row. Different people were asked to observe different segments of the row and describe "cause" from their own perspectives.

Stephen described the cause-and-effect chain of events in a rhythmic chant I found rather appealing. The point of it was to show that each person (except the one at the end of the row) was either cause or effect, depending on the place from which you looked. Actually, no one in the row was at cause, since Stephen had been the source of the original push. Rather, they each were *effect, effect, effect, effect, effect, effect, effect.*

Another physical demonstration followed with Sandy, one of the volunteers from the effect line who remained on stage. Stephen had Sandy straighten her arm, hold it up over her head, and then bring it down on his shoulder. He ran through a list of possible ways of handling this. The first would be to resist, in which case one would be bent into the shape of the blow. (I got that this statement was intended to be heavy with symbolism.) One could also avoid the blow and run away, but this would in all likelihood only lead to pursuit. Or one could remain in place and be the victim. None of these were great ideas so far, but there were better choices made available. One could create a space for the blow, just by stepping aside. One could go to source, by pushing through

one's own shoulder just as the other's hand made contact. One could, ultimately, engage in sourcing—
that word I detested for its Newspeak sound. Sourcing would be exemplified by using momentum to step
around behind the initiator of the blow. This sounded
familiar. I thought I remembered something similar
from a judo course I had taken when I lived on the
south side of Chicago.

Next there was a lecture about children, the nature thereof. Children were described as adults in
little bodies. They play only one game, the one called
Domination. Children are little, we were reminded,
and have to survive. If you support them totally they
can give up their game. Children respect rules naturally. This was illustrated by what I was coming to
view as a typically estian tactic of reasoning by analogy. This was it: After all, gravity is the master rulemaker and children learn to walk, *don't* they? So
here was the way to handle them. One: Make definite rules. Two: Don't explain. To this last commandment was added the explanation that children are
master logicians and one would inevitably lose any attempts to engage them on their own turf.

Now that we had mastered child rearing we were
given an opportunity to share our view of what constituted Mind, before est laid it on us the following
day. The microphones were passed from person to
person, down each row. Anyone who wanted to, and
almost everybody did, was given a chance to say what

he or she thought Mind is. There were lots of suggestions: a computer, a camera, a filing cabinet, the brain, myself, the means through which we apprehend reality. When it got to be my turn I said that one of the few things I knew for sure was that I *didn't know* what the mind is. My comment was the symptom of an occupational disease. The more you study, the less you know. Too bad that empty head isn't compensatible like black lung.

Now we were in for a humorous interval, called Being an Asshole. This section of the evening—and it was evening by then—was introduced by the comment that one's fear of being an asshole causes one to seek agreement (from others). The only way not to be run by one's assholeness was to stop pretending *not* to be an asshole. All those in the training who had not yet shared or asked a question were labeled as those who were most afraid of being an asshole. Everyone in this category had to come to the front of the room, as many as possible standing on the stage and the rest dribbling off the sides. Following the example set by Stephen, we all had to act out the following skit with gestures and *expression:*

You wake up in the morning with a terrific hangover. You have to decide whether to risk moving or have your bladder explode. You bite the bullet and stagger to the bathroom, where you discover your mangled toothbrush which your son has used to brush the teeth of the family's Saint Bernard. You yell,

Don't you ever, ever, EVER let ME catch YOU using MY TOOTHBRUSH on that dog again! We did it at least three times before we had satisfied Stephen that we were really putting out, one hundred percent.

The second skit we did had much more enthusiastic performances from the start. The first group was allowed to retreat from the stage. In turn all the women in the room and all the men in the room had to do separate skits, in place at their chairs, while they were observed by the opposite sex. After one run-through on the skit, an audition, anyone whose performance had been judged inadequate by *anyone* in the audience had to go to the stage and perform the skit until they did it *perfectly*. Most people managed the transition from embarrassment to enjoyment with apparent ease.

We were given a meal break around 11 P.M. When we came back we did a process that seemed to be an exercise of our increasing ability to experience experience. (Why did they keep saying things *twice* in est? I kept thinking, "New York, New York. If we didn't love it, we wouldn't have named it twice." Yech.) Under our chairs were two plastic bags. In one were a metal cube, a wood cube, and a smooth stone. In the other were a cherry tomato, a strawberry, and a wedge of lemon. Next to the plastic bags was a daisy.

Stephen instructed us to sense each object. We

looked, smelled, felt, and heard the sound of the two cubes as they clapped together. The vegetables we tasted on several different parts of our tongue. We experienced the tomato seeds. We passed the used materials over to the aisles, where they were collected. Lying down, we went into our spaces. Then we stood up and did a guided fantasy journey into a fifteen-foot-tall vegetable, experiencing it with all our senses. A sixty-five-foot daisy was next on our itinerary. We climbed up through the stem and came out through the center to play upon the petals. Then we did the Mexican Hat Dance. On top of a sixty-five-foot daisy. With our eyes closed. Surrounded by two hundred fifty other people. In the Gold Ballroom of the Statler Hilton.

The next process was Creating Your Center. This was a place inside your space which you could create exactly according to your own intentions. It was to have a chair with a wish-switch, two other chairs on either side, a desk with a video cassette and a phone, and a three-part library. The library contained film cassettes of situations in which you wanted to manifest perfection, books on topics of which you wanted to have total knowledge, and files on people you wanted information about. There was to be an opaque compartment with a door that slid open vertically. Next to the compartment was a platform, or stage. In the middle of the center (I *know*, but that's the way it is in est) was a screen. Nearby was a door through which you could enter the scene on the screen. Finally, there was a cabinet of abilities in which were hung the appropriate suits to put on when you needed specialized skills.

Standing up, with our eyes closed, we acted out the construction of this empire. We chose the location, materials, and shape of things. Then we invited into our centers two people, a man and a woman. We created each of these people in our imaginations, sculpting their bodies and manufacturing them to the last detail. We held conversations with each of them, saying out loud whatever came to mind. We were the scriptwriters, directors, and cameramen. We could make this little movie in our minds come out any way we wanted it to.

When our conversations were complete, we opened our eyes and went home.

9

You Got It

AFTER A REFRESHING FOUR HOURS of sleep I reappeared at the Statler Hilton. Sunday morning seemed an appropriate time to receive the revelation of the nature of the mind. This lecture, entitled the Anatomy of the Mind, started off with a reminder that the brain is part of the mind. Long before this, I had made a decision to stop *thinking* about the information put out in the est training. I followed instructions and took what I got. Part of what I got is that the mind *is* "a linear arrangement of multisensory *total* recordings of successive moments of now." I have condensed into one sentence the contents of more than an hour of lecture. Memorize that sentence and you'd get a Ph.D. in estian psychology.

The mind has a purpose, in the sense of its design form. The purpose and only purpose of the mind is *survival*. Survival refers to survival of the self or the being or whatever the self considers itself to be. When one's being is identified with the mind, the necessary conditions are created for a mode of functioning called "Ego." If "Being" is a circle and "Mind" is a square, we were told, "Ego" is a square containing a circle. Survival then means survival of the mind, which means seeing itself everywhere and invalidating any other point of view. Thus: Self-righteousness. The necessity of self-righteousness for the survival of the mind results in being concerned with dominating and avoiding domination, with being right and not wrong, with winning and not losing, with self-justification and the invalidation of others.

We were told that the self's point of view, or our self-righteousness, is more important even than the survival of one's physical self or body. Thus is explained suicide. It is OK with the mind for us to be dead heroes, carried around forever. We were warned that the mind would try to dominate even this very information. The mind would even try to use est for its own ends, in which case we would have the opportunity of experiencing being an est-hole.

The records that make up the mind are subdivided into those that are necessary and those that are not necessary for survival. Those which are necessary for the survival of the self are records of threats to survival which you survived in the past. There are three categories of such threatening events. Events described as type number one were defined by having involved pain—or impact—and unconsciousness. The unconsciousness did not have to have been absolute, but was a relative concept. In number-one events, the person might have been totally unconscious or might merely have been relatively more unconscious (less conscious?) than in other types of situations. Lest you think that you have been lucky enough to have escaped such situations in your particular life (phew!), the example given of a number-one event was a story of a little boy riding his tricycle down the driveway and crashing in the street.

Number-two incidents are those involving loss or shock. In such situations there is negative emotion or no emotion. Number-three events are unwitting reminders of number ones or number twos. These reminders of earlier threats to survival constitute what Stephen referred to as an "upset." The whole collection of the three kinds of incidents are held in the mind in a linear arrangement; they are all tied together as if on a string. Now it was necessary for us to know that the logic of the mind equals no logic. The mind works by concepts of identity, not on the more sophisticated level of similarities and differences. A dog is a dog is a dog except not always. This is important as an explanation of the reason we react to things in our current environment. When something in the environment is similar to any element on a "string," it pulls in the whole string. Stephen then proceeded to "demonstrate" how many number-one, number-two, and number-three incidents we have accumulated. The answer was trillions. The conclusion, and it was a conclusion, is that we are totally controlled and mechanical. Each of us is *effect, effect, effect, effect, effect, effect*. Nary a *cause* in sight.

I don't know how long it had been since the Anatomy of the Mind began on Sunday morning, but it seemed like months. The message that one is *totally controlled*, a machine, led on to the climax of the whole training. Stephen asked, "Who got it?" There was a moment or two of quiet hesitation. Then, by a show of hands, we separated ourselves into three groups: those who got it, those who were sure they hadn't gotten it, and those who weren't sure or didn't know. Clearly a majority had gotten it, about sixty percent of the people in the room. Another large group was sure they hadn't gotten it. They were congratulated. If you're certain that you don't know, then— *you got it*. The only ones remaining were ten or twelve people who had indicated they weren't sure whether they got it or not. I admired their courage, standing up there in the audience surrounded by two hundred forty other people, most of whom were in some sort of giggly state of exhilaration. Stephen went around to each person who was unsure, one by one, and asked them to change what they were doing when they were doing it. It went something like this:

"Barbara, what are you doing now?"

"I'm standing."

"Good. You're standing. Now I'd like you to sit when you're standing." Barbara sat down. *"Now,* what are you doing?"

"I'm sitting."

"Good. You're sitting. Now stand up. Now sit down. Can you sit when you're standing? Can you stand when you're sitting? *No,* you can only do what you're doing when you're doing it. *You got it.* Congratulations."

You can't change the now. Do what you're doing when you're doing it. Whatever is going on for you, create it. Choose it. You might as well.

Enlightenment is that state where you get better at realizing when a string is being pulled in. You then have an instant of choice. Choice for est transcends any considerations one has concerning the relative desirability of one alternative over any other alternative. This principle was painfully demonstrated by a volunteer from the audience who joined Stephen on the stage to display the nature of choice. Her name was Jennifer.

Stephen: Jennifer, I'd like you to choose chocolate or vanilla.

Jennifer: I choose chocolate.

Stephen: Jennifer, why did you choose chocolate?

Jennifer: I chose chocolate because I like it better.

Stephen: No, Jennifer. That's not a choice, it's a decision based on your considerations about the relative value of chocolate and vanilla. Try again. Choose chocolate or vanilla.

Jennifer: Vanilla.

Stephen: Why did you choose vanilla?

Jennifer: I chose vanilla because I thought you'd yell at me again if I chose chocolate.

Stephen: No, Jennifer, try it again. Chocolate or vanilla.

Jennifer: (tentatively, this time) Vanilla.

Stephen: Why?

Jennifer: I chose vanilla . . . because I really like chocolate and you know that by now so I took the opposite.

Stephen: Jennifer, we're going to stay here until you get it. Choose chocolate or vanilla.

Jennifer: Chocolate. Because it tastes good.

Stephen: Choose chocolate or vanilla, Jennifer.

This went on for what felt like hours. I wanted to hit her. Eventually she got it.

Jennifer: I chose chocolate because I chose chocolate.

Stephen: And what if you had chosen vanilla?

Jennifer: Then I would have chosen vanilla because I chose vanilla.

There was enthusiastic applause from the audience. Thank God, we're home at last.

Stephen then returned to the subject of enlightenment. He warned us that we would oscillate between experiencing and nonexperiencing. Enlightenment is not continuous. He wrote the words BE, DO, and HAVE on the blackboard. An antimaterialist lecture on the ultimate meaninglessness of *things* followed. Most people think you start out with *having* the things appropriate to whatever it is you're concerned with eventually being. So if you want to be a skier, you first have to *have* skis and boots and poles and the right kind of parka and pants and hat and gloves and a house at the right resort. Then you *do* the things that skiers do, like go to Aspen. Then you get to *be* a skier. *Wrong.* It works the other way around. First you choose *to be* a skier, then you do the things skiers do, then you have the things skiers have.

There were a few more topics to cover before the lectures would end. There was a section on relationships and the nature of love. There was a demonstration that life is a game and we make the rules. It was clear that the way to transform your life was simply to change your point of view. You could have Righteousness. *Or* you could have Aliveness.

We were told that some est graduates had come to the hotel that evening to participate in the graduation ceremony which would be the final event of the training. We would now have the chance to meet these graduates. The doors to the training room were thrown open. In marched a parade of the graduates, in

single or double file. They were all clapping, hands
held over their heads, smiles stretching across their
cheeks. There were more than a hundred of them.
They stood all along the back and sides of the room
and clapped and clapped. Then Stephen motioned
for quiet and suggested that we might want to acknowledge the graduates. The two hundred fifty
trainees began to clap. The applause went on and on
and on. Everyone was totally enthusiastic.

The graduates then left to prepare for the final
ceremony. We were detained in the training room,
with a little more lecturing and instructions concerning
how we were to enter the graduation room. This second room, an adjacent ballroom, was set up so that
two of us sat facing one of the graduates who had
come to assist. The graduate took each of us through
a Personality Profile, similar to the demonstration
Debbie had performed at the Pre-Training Seminar.
When we completed the Profile, if we were satisfied
with our own performance, we were to raise our
hands. Stephen then came over to make a personal
visit to each outstretched hand and tell us, "Congratulations. You're an est graduate."

The Post-Training Seminar was held the following
Wednesday evening. It was led by Stephen, who had
flown back to New York from the West Coast only an
hour or so before the meeting began. We had been invited to bring friends, and I had brought along a col-

league with whom I had had a few conversations about
est during the period over the last two weeks when I
had been involved in the training. The Post-Training
began with sharing. There were all the usual testimonials: diseases cured, relationships mended, jobs improved, attitudes changed, pleasures increased, and
pains diminished.

John, my guest, leaned over toward me and asked,
"Why are all these people clapping every time somebody says something?" I tried to explain that it was a
norm, a custom in est to acknowledge that you have
received a communication. He looked a little puzzled
and I felt a little embarrassed. Then it was time for the
guests to leave, in small groups assigned to one of the
Guest Seminar leaders, so that they could have a
chance to hear about the est training and ask questions.
The rest of the Post-Training for us new graduates
consisted of hearing more about the graduate program and signing up for the seminars that would start
us off on our postgraduate careers. I filled out a card
stating that I did not intend to enroll in a seminar.
Soon my name was called and I walked over to the
registration table. I had the impression that "no" was
an answer they weren't used to hearing. The volunteer
handling my case asked me why I wasn't registering. I
made the mistake of trying to justify my refusal with a
reference to my overburdened schedule. This bought
me five minutes of grilling on the details of my commitments. "Are you busy *every* evening of the week?"

queried the registrar, as though she had made me an offer I couldn't refuse. In desperation, I took an est tactic. "No. I do not want to take a seminar next semester *and* I might decide to do so in the future." She smiled and I was free to return to my seat.

When we were dismissed I walked out into the hotel lobby to find John. There was an expression on his face that I interpreted as incredulity. I asked him how he had liked it. He talked about the "miracles" his seminar leader had said were part of her life after taking est.

"She said that she never has to wait for the subway any more. Now, when she walks into the station, the train comes on time."

By the time I graduated I had a book to write. My description of the training was written from notes during my Christmas vacation while the experience was fresh. I took some time to reflect upon est and what it meant and then began the analysis which follows.

Part II:

THE QUESTIONS

10

Is est Brainwashing?

BRAINWASHING HAS BECOME a popular term since it was first coined by a reporter to refer to Chinese Communist efforts at "thought reform" of American prisoners during the Korean war. Public concern over "brainwashing" was again stimulated by Patty Hearst's kidnapping and subsequent conversion to the cause of her captors. Religious cults, based on following the teachings of one guru or another, have attracted young adherents whose parents have sometimes hired "deprogrammers" to rescue their offspring from a life of zealotry. *fanatical devotion*

In an article in *Psychology Today*,* the est training was referred to as brainwashing. Spokespersons for est have on a variety of occasions denied this charge to the media or to groups of trainees. I see little to be gained through this sort of name-calling and would

* See pp. 183ff for bibliographic notes for Part II.

suggest instead that we accept at face value for the moment the stated purpose of est as being a "transformation." Going beyond this, and ignoring the idiosyncratic use of language which is so characteristic of the est training, a psychological view of their aims would describe the purpose of est as being changes in beliefs, attitudes, and behavior. They do this through "manipulation," which merely means planned, purposeful actions intended to produce a desired effect. This process is, in other contexts, referred to as persuasion and is encountered every day by human beings who interact with other human beings, either in the flesh or through spoken, written, or televised messages. Persuaders, hidden or otherwise, are a pervasive fact of life. They're everywhere—in the schools, in the churches, among your friends, on the airwaves—and their purposes are varied: to influence you to think a thought, believe a belief, perform an act, buy a product, contribute to a charity, or reelect the president.

Attempts at influence and persuasion literally surround us; we become concerned about them only when we think they work—and we don't like the message—or when we think agreement has been obtained coercively. Is the est training a coercive persuasion? The criteria for coercion suggested by social psychologist Philip Zimbardo include: (1) dramatic conversions which occur suddenly rather than gradually evolving, (2) control of information, (3) intensity of

peculiar construction

contact with agents of influence, (4) isolation from or limited contact with one's former sources of approval or reality testing, and (5) a promise of eventual relief.

Is this the est training? More or less. Any conversions—or "transformations"—that occur in the space of two weekends would be viewed as relatively sudden, by all usual standards. Information is certainly tightly controlled: Trainees have no watches during the training; est staff members and volunteers, whether assisting at trainings or making phone calls from the est office, have tightly programmed responses; "spontaneous" anecdotes are written out in advance for memorization by seminar leaders.

There's also no question that the est training is an intensive experience in which contact with persuasive agents is prolonged beyond the limits of a typical evening's entertainment. While the usual sources of information are not literally inaccessible, you don't have the *time* to see much of family and friends while undergoing the training, and, in addition, your usual sources have largely been discredited because they are very likely operating from such unenlightened positions as that of "reasonableness." Finally, the discomfort and confusion is made endurable only by the promise of "getting it" in the afternoon of the second Sunday of the training.

Coercion is not *necessary* to bring about changes in the ways we think, feel, and act, nor does it often have effects which are more than temporary. The est training is too cleverly constructed to rely on coercive measures. Instead, trainers continually make use of well-known principles of attitude and behavior change, calculated to have trainees identify with and internalize the training rather than merely to comply. The whole training is composed of such manipulations. Let's look at some specific examples so we can see how it works.

One principle of behavior influence that makes a frequent appearance in est is known as the "foot-in-the-door" technique. People are more likely to agree to a large request if they have first agreed to comply with a small one. Participation in the est training involves a progressive series of commitments. Most people begin by hearing about est from their friends and agreeing to attend a Guest Seminar. At the Guest Seminar you *may* enroll in the training if you like, or you may just sign a card and give them your address and phone number. If you have signed the card—only a minor commitment in itself—you later receive a call asking if you are interested in the training. If you are interested in the training, you are increasingly "encouraged" to make a decision to sign up. Each act along the way increases the probability that you will agree to the next request. This is not "forced compliance." It just means that, for the most part, we *infer* our own feelings and attitudes by observing our own behavior or the environment in which we are operating.

Two examples are often cited as illustrations of this phenomenon. The first example is something you might be able to observe in your friends. Imagine this scene: You are working with George and have been absorbed in a project for an entire morning. After some hours have gone by, you ask George if he's hungry. His response is to look at his watch. He checks for *external cues* to give him information about an internal state.

Second example: You ask someone if she likes Chinese food. Her response, which may or may not be something she verbalizes out loud to you, might go something like this: "I guess I do, I eat it all the time." Although people are to different degrees aware of the extent to which they do this, there is considerable reason to believe that we *infer* our likes and dislikes by observing the things we do or avoid doing.

In est, the progressive agreements to do small things such as putting your name and phone number on a card make it more likely that you will later agree to larger requests. As you comply at each stage, you "rearrange" your attitudes to account for your behavior. If I went to a Guest Seminar, I must want to give them my name. If I give them my name, I must be interested in hearing more about the training. If I'm interested in more information, eventually I'll take the training. If not now, when?

Related to this is another powerful attitude-change technique. This one is based on the human need to justify our actions to ourselves. If we, for example, feel that we have in some way been "forced" to listen to a speech, we are not very likely to change our attitudes toward the speaker or toward the subject matter. If we had negative views before, we are not likely to become more positive *even if* the pitch is a convincing one. This is because we need no further justification for our behavior under conditions of perceived coercion. We might say to ourselves something like: "I'm just here to make my husband happy" or "I *had* to come—my friend would never have let me hear the end of it if I didn't." Most of us like to think of ourselves as people who in some way fulfill the expectations of others who are important to us, and this in itself is reason enough for our behavior.

The power of this mechanism is illustrated and recognized in the est training in the lecture on child-rearing techniques. The trainer tells you that the way to bring up children is: (1) Make definite rules and (2) Don't explain. The second admonition is sound psychology. If you don't give people reasons, they have to invent their own and in the process of doing so will choose the explanation that to them is most convincing. It would go like this: "If I'm doing this, there must be a good reason. What could it be? Maybe I *like* it. Hey, that's it! I *must* like it or I wouldn't be doing it." If people have the impression they have voluntarily committed themselves to an action, they will increase their liking for that action and will be more likely to internalize the attitudes, standards, or values that their action has implied. The opportunities throughout the est training to leave and receive a full refund are brilliant manipulations of this effect. Your sense of having made a voluntary commitment to be there is bolstered. You *could* have left but you didn't, and if you didn't then you must want to be there. Once you have convinced yourself that you are there because you want to be, your receptivity to the content of the message is at a high point.

The psychological impact of the seemingly arbitrary rules works in much the same way. No reasons are given. Since most of us do not think of ourselves as people who slavishly follow orders, we provide reasons for ourselves: "This is fun" or "It's good for my character" or "I'll do this to show how strong I am." Once having adhered to the prescriptions, we rationalize that they were really not so burdensome after all or that it was tough but immensely worthwhile.

You can easily see that people's overall reactions to the training would also make use of such mechanisms. If you've paid $250, spent two weekends and three week nights of your time, and endured deprivations and insults, you'd better find reasons to like it.

Est doesn't need to "brainwash" people. We all do it for ourselves every day.

11

Is est Psychotherapy?

THE APPLICATION FORM filled out by all those who
take the est training states that the training is "not
psychotherapeutic in nature." But if it is "not psychotherapeutic in nature," what is it?

On the cover of the first est publication one re-
ceives after enrolling in the training are the definitions
of four words: happiness, love, health, and self-expression. How reasonable to assume that the training has
something to do with altering one's attitudes or behavior related to happiness, love, health, and/or
self-expression. And to the extent that psychotherapy
refers to specific procedures designed to change attitudes and behavior with the goal of increased well-
being, it is mere equivocation to insist that the est
training is not a type of psychotherapy.

It would be convenient to compare the est training with a short, concise, complete, and generally acceptable definition of psychotherapy. However, the

124

field is so varied that no one simple definition can include the vast array of techniques, applied to a wide variety of psychological problems, that seem to fall within the domain of one or another school of psychotherapy. A dictionary definition of psychotherapy describes it as the "science or art of curing psychological abnormalities and disorders by psychological techniques." Even this definition, specifying neither the techniques nor the disorders to which they are applied, would be too narrow to encompass the variety of activities pursued by psychotherapists today.

The domain of psychotherapy has broadened steadily since the days of Sigmund Freud, who was initially concerned only with a narrowly defined group of "hysterical" patients suffering from substantially disabling complaints (such as blindness) or paralyses which resembled neurological disorders. Psychotherapy today is a heterogeneous collection of techniques, applied by practitioners with diverse theories, working with patients (or clients) who may or may not show "impairment" in the usual sense of the word, and the goals of those who seek help vary widely, ranging from the wish to eliminate a single symptom in a brief period of treatment to open-ended hopes for increased self-knowledge and satisfaction in life.

Much of the contents of the est training are subjects of interest to psychologists: emotions, sensations, perception, behavior, personal distress, the nature of the mind. My experience with it suggests that it has as many similarities to psychotherapy as various current types of psychotherapy—psychoanalytic psychotherapy, cognitive-behavioral therapy, Gestalt therapy, existential psychotherapy, humanistic psychotherapy, client-centered counseling—have to each other.

I asked a fellow psychologist who is an est graduate for his opinion of the psychotherapeutic nature of est. He replied with the following anecdotes:

In the first weekend of the training, on Sunday, the trainer spent sixteen hours doing therapy the whole time. He did it in a masterful way. If he had done that demonstration at a hospital or if you could do that for a psychotherapy class, it would be the most exciting, clearest demonstration of general principles of psychotherapy I've ever seen. There's no question that est is psychotherapy. Here are some examples.

One girl said that her hip had been hurting her for years and years. In the first night of the training she had been thinking about her hip as she got into her 'hip space' in the processes. She realized that when she was young she had had an operation on her hip that she had completely forgotten about. In the training, she remembered the whole operation vividly.

A heavy woman with blond hair, maybe forty or forty-five years old, stood up. She started off not quite saying anything, stating, "I don't know why I got up. It's not clear what I want to say." She went on for a while and her story was this. Her brother had committed suicide. He had previously been hospitalized for several psychotic episodes. He had attacked her and beaten her up and tried to kill her once. The brother was older than she. There was some concern that the brother might be going to move back into the house with the family. He came to visit them at the house. She saw that he was seriously disturbed and in danger of "flipping out" again. Instead of reaching out to him, she went up to her room and talked to a friend on the telephone. Four days later her brother committed suicide.

She felt that she had, in a way, killed her brother. Then she went into a long discussion of whether she loved her brother or didn't love her brother, whether she hated her brother. She started to cry. Much to my amazement, the trainer did not back off when she started to cry. He pursued her vigorously. This was quite early in the morning, right in the beginning of the second day of the training. He made her go through a whole routine that she was in fact responsible for her brother's death, that she had killed him. The trainer was calling her a shit and saying that it was her fault. She protested and said she hadn't forced her brother, she hadn't held the gun to his head or pulled the trigger. The trainer kept after her, insisting that she was responsible for the death, and finally she was crying and saying yes, that she had killed her brother.

The trainer asked her other questions about her life and there were several other tragedies and crises. For each one, he took her through a gamut of emotions and said that she was responsible for all of it and that she had to accept that.

He used her as an example all morning and kept referring back to things she had said. I thought she was really in trouble. Well, maybe not *really* in trouble because I could see that she had quite a bit of strength. But she was crying and was obviously very distressed. The trainer was using her as an example more than he was helping her. It surprised me how relentlessly he pursued her. The closure of it was that she could realize that she really had hated her brother. She could also realize that, underneath that hate, she had loved her brother. By completing the experience, her guilt about it would disappear. The trainer told her that it would take time to complete this and that it would be coming apart for her, maybe over the next week and maybe over the next year.

The woman talking about her brother evidently set the pace. For the next four hours, people confessed to the most incredible range of things. The trainer pursued most of them to get them to take responsibility for having created the worst thing in their life, or the things they felt were worst about themselves.

It seemed as though everyone was crying all day in this training. People were also gagging and throwing up. A man who had seemed hostile on the first day and had asked the trainer if he needed to be so nasty, just fell apart while he was standing in the lineup. I don't know if he was dramatizing it or not, although it was certainly dramatic. He started screaming and crying out loud. This lasted for what must have been an hour. Even when he got back to his seat he continued crying and screaming and throwing up in a bag.

Two seats down from him someone else was throwing up and also screaming.

You could say this wasn't psychotherapy, in the best sense of the word. I'm certainly not saying that I think these people were necessarily helped or that the effects of what they went through, or were put through, were therapeutic in the sense of being beneficial. Est may not be psychotherapy, but I find it unbelievable that it could be considered to be "education" or some kind of philosophical training. Is education supposed to concern itself with guilt over a brother's suicide?

Is est psychotherapy? If it walks like a duck and it talks like a duck, then it might well be a platypus. But the odds are, if you're not at the zoo, it's a duck.

12

Why Do They Train 250 People at Once?

WHY ARE EST TRAININGS conducted with such large groups of people? So the organization can take in $62,500 for two weekends. But even if the economics of the situation weren't quite so attractive, there would still be sound psychological reasons for doing it in a crowd. Ever since Aristotle, human beings have been described as social animals. The influence people have on the behavior of others is a well-studied phenomenon. A good deal of what we know about social influence suggests that the effects of something like the est training are greatly enhanced by the group setting.

In 1896 a Frenchman named Le Bon wrote a book which in the English translation was called *The Crowd*. He observed that people in groups behave quite differently than they would when alone. Individuals begin to feel invincible in groups because they are anonymous. Responsibility is diffused. Feelings, thoughts, and actions are contagious. Le Bon compared the condition of an individual in a group to that of a hypnotic subject. He thought that people become more suggestible and impulsive under the influence of the "group mind." He observed that the individual's capacity for critical thought is reduced in the group. Le Bon said, "Isolated, he may be a cultivated individual; in a crowd, he is a barbarian."

A group has the power to stir people emotionally. According to Le Bon, man in a crowd "possesses the spontaneity, the violence, the ferocity, and also the enthusiasm and heroism of primitive beings." McDougall, too, writing in 1920 about *The Group Mind*, noted the "exaltation or intensification of emotion" produced in every individual transformed into a member of a group.

In recent years social psychologists have conducted a number of experiments which allow us to specify the mechanisms and extent of social influence without having to resort to vague concepts such as the "group mind." In a classic set of experiments, Solomon Asch demonstrated the influence of group opinion in bringing about conformity. The situation created by Asch called for subjects to make a basic perceptual judgment. They were shown a straight line and then three other lines with which to compare the first one. Their task was simple: to indicate which of the three lines was closest in length to the first one. When the subjects were alone, there were almost no

errors in their performance. The judgment was an
easy one; there were no optical illusions or "tricks"
which would make the actual lengths of the lines
difficult to determine.

When subjects were asked to make their judgments in a group setting, however, the results were
very different. The experiment was set up in such
a way that the other members of the group were con-
federates of the experimeter. They each answered
first and they answered incorrectly. When it came to
be the turn of the true experimental subject, about
a third of these people conformed to the group consensus rather than stick with their own clear perceptual judgments, and later experiments demonstrated
that conformity increased as the perceptual judgment
was made more difficult and subjects became less confident of their own accuracy.

Does this demonstration of conformity to the
perceptual judgments of others have anything to do
with what goes on in the est training? Other researchers interested in further investigation of conformity
have looked at other kinds of group influence and
demonstrated that group consensus can result in the
acceptance of totally absurd statements and personal
and political opinions. Social pressure influences people to conform to the judgments of a group. Ac-
cepting the opinions of the est trainer, acquiescing
to philosophical principles espoused in the training,
and judging the value of the experience are all phe-

nomena which we would expect to be enhanced by the fact of the group setting.

In the Asch conformity experiments, it was thought likely that people change their judgments to agree with the group in order to obtain the rewards of social approval or avoid the punishment of social ostracism. But other factors besides the desire for reward or the fear of punishment operate to make us susceptible to the views or behavior of others. The influence of these other factors extends even to the ways in which we assess our own feelings. We'll take a look at this particular process in the next question when we look at the effects of deprivation in the est training.

13

Why Won't They Let You Go to the Bathroom?

THE BATHROOM RESTRICTIONS are only one of many aspects of the est training which add up to the fact that the training takes place in a state of deprivation. During the training you are deprived of sleep because you arrive home around 3 A.M. and have to be back at the hotel by 8:30 the next morning. A typical training session that took place in February 1976 began at 8:30 on a Saturday morning. The first break occurred at 2:30 in the afternoon. This was a bathroom break when consumption of liquids was allowed but no food was to be taken. A second bathroom break was allowed at 8:30 P.M. The dinner break occurred at about midnight. People who smoke were undergoing additional deprivation; there was no smoking in the training room so cigarettes were unavailable for six-hour periods. Distractions such as reading, taking notes, chewing gum, talking, or doing busywork were not allowed. The typical means by which people bind or reduce tension were unavailable.

Many of the deprivations, such as the restriction on bathroom privileges, could be expected to have the effect of creating anxiety. For many people, the extensive rules and their authoritarian enforcement might be expected to create anger. Anger and anxiety are both states of emotional arousal. Deprivation creates arousal, which under such conditions is referred to as motivation. If you want to teach a rat to run in a maze, you deprive it of food so you can control its behavior by doling out food when it does what you want it to do.

Emotional arousal is thought to be one of the necessary preconditions for therapeutic movement or susceptibility to the influence of another. People undergoing the est training might experience arousal for any one of a number of reasons, but it is clear that arousal will be amplified by the deprivation state in which the training takes place. Other aspects of the manner in which the training is conducted also contribute to a loss of the benchmarks by which we normally monitor our environments and ourselves. One's sense of time is distorted because there are no cues: Watches and clocks are not allowed in the training room, and the physical setting itself is an anonymous hotel ballroom with artificial light and no windows to the outdoors. Physical reality becomes unclear. Combined with the intense arousal, this has powerful effects on the way in which we perceive even our own feelings.

What are "feelings" composed of? According to William James, the great nineteenth-century American psychologist, emotions have two components, a "feeling" aspect and a "thought" aspect. The feeling aspect is a physiological change, a response of the sympathetic nervous system. It is a state of being "churned up" marked by increases in heart rate, accelerated breathing, and perhaps tremors, flushing, and perspiration.

Physiologist Walter Cannon cited evidence indicating that different emotions are accompanied by much the *same* physiological state. Spurred on by this suggestion, psychologists began to investigate the "thought" aspect of emotion. The "feeling" or physiological arousal which we experience gets *interpreted* by us—this is the "thought" aspect—partly in terms of what we see in our environment. The environment provides us with cues with which to interpret the arousal we are feeling. If you feel aroused and are watching a horror movie, you are likely to interpret your arousal as fear. If for some reason it is unacceptable to you to admit to being afraid, you might interpret your arousal as humor and laugh as Lon Chaney transmogrifies into Wolfman at the rising of the full moon.

The point is this: Fear, anger, euphoria, and exhilaration are all very similar physiologically. We are aroused. When the physical reality is unclear, the behavior of other people becomes a vital source of information. It has been demonstrated that the influence of others extends even to the way in which we interpret what we are feeling.

So one of the effects of the deprivation-induced arousal people experience in the est training is to facilitate the influence of the group. The extent of this influence was documented in one of the most important psychological experiments in recent history, conducted by Stanley Schachter and Jerome Singer. In this experiment, subjects were injected with epinephrine, a synthetic form of adrenaline which causes physiological arousal or excitation of the sympathetic nervous system. The subjects were uninformed about the symptoms they might expect; they thought they had received a vitamin supplement and expected no "side effects." Some of these subjects were placed in an experimental room in the company of another "subject" who was actually a stooge of the experimenters. If the stooge began to act extremely annoyed, to complain about a questionnaire that was part of the experiment, and eventually to rip up the questionnaire and angrily hurl it into the wastebasket, the real subjects began to act angrily and later to report that they *felt* angry. If the stooge behaved euphorically, bounc-

ing around the room and acting with abandon, subjects began to behave happily and to report feeling
euphoric.

If you are feeling aroused in the est training and
other people are giving testimonials as to the miracles
in their life, or their feelings of being transformed,
it is very likely that you too will interpret your "feelings" in a similar manner.

It is also likely that the deprivations caused by the
rules enforced during the training contribute to the
establishment of the trainer's authority and thus add to
the effectiveness of the est training. The authority of
the leader of a group has been demonstrated to be
important in bringing about attitude change; the development of faith in a healer is thought to be an important component (perhaps *the* important component) in therapeutic improvement. And the power
the trainer holds over trainees is likely to be increased
by the gratitude one feels when he finally allows a
break.

14

Does est Work?

IN THE DESCRIPTION in chapter 9 of the Post-Training Seminar held at the conclusion of the second weekend of my est training, I mentioned the testimonials I heard: diseases cured, relationships mended, jobs improved, attitudes changed, pleasures increased, and pains diminished. Are these testimonials good evidence of the effects of the est training? Two other questions underlie this one. First, if people say they are in some way "better off," have they actually changed or are they just "saying so"? Second, if *real* changes are somehow established and measured, are they owing to the est training or to other factors which may be coincidental with taking the training?

There are no published scientific studies to provide us with the information we need to answer these questions. However, we can still draw some informed tentative conclusions, based on two sources of information: information on est graduates contained in

two unpublished reports, which we shall review, and
a large collection of research on the outcome of various modes of psychotherapy, which we can compare
and contrast with the est training.

The first report is dated May 29, 1973, and is
titled "Abstract of the Behaviordyne Report on Psychological Changes Measured After Taking the Erhard Seminars Training." According to this summary,
a personality test was administered to persons enrolled in an est training before they began the training, at the end of the training, and three months following the training. The test given was the California
Psychological Inventory, a standard test developed for
use with so-called normal populations and designed to
assess favorable and positive aspects of personality
rather than psychological problems or personality
difficulties.

It is important to note that the *results* of these
tests are not reported in the summary, but only the
authors' *interpretations* of the results, a process where
subjective judgments are most directly called for. The
authors conclude that positive changes were found in
those people completing the est training and that these
positive changes were maintained for the three-month
period of follow-up. The specific nature of these
changes is not detailed, but the authors cite a few
statements which suggested to them that people are
"happier," have a better self-image, and feel less anxiety, guilt, and fear after the est training.

It is unfortunate that the full results were not reported in this abstract, because the California Psychological Inventory is constructed in such a manner that we might, were all the data available, be able to answer some of the questions which this abstract leaves unanswered. There are, for example, internal checks within the test itself which assist in detecting those persons who deliberately or otherwise exaggerate their responses. Attempts to portray oneself in an exaggeratedly favorable light can be detected through looking at the person's responses to particular sets of items. This kind of validity check, which is one of the major benefits of using a test such as the California Psychological Inventory, is unfortunately not applied by the authors of this report in their abstract, and we cannot run such checks on our own because the data are not available.

We therefore do not know if the est trainees who participated in all three phases of this study were perhaps those people who are inclined to put their best feet forward. It should be noted, however, that *something* distinguished the people who remained in this study from those who did not. The abstract reports that the study was begun with the testing of 227 persons at the beginning of the est training; at the conclusion of the training, only 144 of these persons were available for testing; and at the end of the three-month follow-up period, this number had shrunk to 93. For some reason, 60 percent of the original trainees did not continue to participate in this research. Were those people who did continue to participate somehow different in their views? There is no way to know.

Another survey of est graduates is referred to as the "Outcome Study" and was reported in summary form by Robert Ornstein and Charles Swencionis, in a memorandum dated June 24, 1975. This report summarizes the results from questionnaires and interviews with some 1,400 est graduates. The authors conclude, again with no presentation of the data on which their observations and interpretations are based, that participants in this study reported "strong, positive" changes in their psychological health and in physical symptoms which are known to have a substantial psychological component. They also reported reductions in the use of various drugs, including pain medication, sleeping pills, tranquilizers, alcohol, marijuana, and cigarettes.

The authors of this report note that their research was not a demonstration of *actual* changes in people's health, but only of changes that people reported they *perceived* in their lives. Since measures of self-reported health status were not taken *before* the training and compared to self-reports *after* the est training, it is incorrect to speak of *changes* that occurred, even when we are accompanying such statements with cautions to the effect that these are merely *perceived* changes. One would have to have measured people's feelings about the state of their health on at least two occasions to speak of *change*.

The "Outcome Study" represents a muffed opportunity. It was certainly no small effort to obtain, process, and analyze the responses from some 1,400 est graduates, but the data obtained tell us very little. Without much more trouble or expense, the study could have been designed to measure actual change, to compare changes in est graduates' lives to changes in the lives of people who had not taken the training or who had pursued other methods of self-improvement, and to obtain some data independent of mere self-reports. One could, for example, have chosen a small subsample of the total group and brought them into a laboratory to obtain much more direct measures of such physiological and behavioral characteristics as anxiety, resistance to stress, reactions to sleep deprivation, and drug consumption, including nicotine and caffeine. Standardized measures of psychological health and adaptive behavior could be included. One could supplement paper-and-pencil tests with actual behavioral assessments of performance. "Personality" factors and mood states could be systematically assessed. Measures of attention, concentration, perceptual discrimination, perceptual-motor coordination, reaction time, learning performance, and short- and long-term recall ability would be of particular interest.

Another important limitation of the "Outcome

Study" is noted by the authors of the report: the fact that reports of "improvements" in one's physical or mental health may be related to the desire shared by most people who answer questionnaires to give responses they think are the appropriate ones. This is known as a "social desirability" effect. The extent of its influence could have been measured by accepted methods and taken into account in the results of this study, but although this problem is mentioned, it was evidently not measured or analyzed.

It is by now a well-known principle of research that both the persons being investigated and the interviewers or experimenters should be uninformed about those aspects of the research that would be expected to influence their responses or interpretations of responses. Psychological experimenters who have particular expectations are likely to find results that confirm their expectations, whether the research subjects are flatworms, rats, college students, or human beings. Given the power of such influences, a power that is well established in psychological research, what do we know about the effects of the est training on the basis of the data available to us? Not much. The reported "improvements" in physical and mental health might reflect merely the participants' wish to give socially appropriate responses. The responses might also reflect the expectations of the experimenters, confirmed either through their own inadvertent error or through subtle "instructions" as to how the participants ought to behave in answering the questionnaire, responding to interview questions, and so forth.

Even if studies were designed to eliminate such possibilities, and it would be relatively easy for a competent researcher to do so, we would be left with still other questions. Suppose, for example, that people reported "real" improvements in self-image after taking the est training. How would we know that those same improvements might not also be found in another group of people who did not take the est training? It is certainly possible that just being asked to participate in a psychological study might give people a sense of importance that would be reflected in increased feelings of self-worth. We would need a *control group* of people who had not taken the est training but who had participated in the testing in order to ascertain whether the very act of studying these people, in and of itself, produced changes in their reported behavior, attitudes, or feelings. We do know from other research that the measuring process itself influences the people being measured. In a classic study of the effects of environmental changes on worker productivity, for example, it was demonstrated that the very introduction of change in *itself* increased productivity, regardless of the specific *nature* of the change.

We have to ask another question: Can we say that it is the training which is responsible for any dif-

ferences we might find between the trainees and a
control group of similar persons who differ from
trainees only in that they have not undergone the
training? Ascertaining the effects of "the training"
would require us to specify just what aspects of the
est experience are considered to be the essential ingredients of change. Is it the fact of paying $250? Is
it sitting in a hotel room for hours on end, two weekends in a row? Is it lack of sleep or food or cigarettes
or liquor? Is it the influence of doing something (anything?) with 250 other people? Is it the content of the
lectures? The appearance and actions of the trainer?
The relaxation brought about by the meditative
states? In order to know, we would have to vary each
of these factors, one at a time, and see if there were
any differences in groups exposed, or not exposed, to
them.

Although we do not have scientifically acceptable
data on the specific effects of the est training, we can
take a look at an extensive collection of studies on the
outcome of psychotherapy. This research has been
argued over by scientists for the last fifteen years,
which allows us to benefit from a great deal of critical
analysis. British psychologist Hans Eysenck initially
suggested that about two thirds of patients improved in either psychoanalysis or eclectic psychotherapy. This figure by itself means nothing, however,
for it is probably quite common for the kinds of
symptoms for which people seek psychotherapy of

this type to clear up spontaneously over the period of time that would, for someone in therapy, constitute the treatment period. Eysenck's data suggested that two thirds of neurotic disabilities cleared up spontaneously, without treatment, over a two-year period, so eclectic therapy or psychoanalysis was said to be no more useful than the effects of time!

These data have been superseded by a more recent and more careful analysis, indicating that eclectic therapy has an improvement rate of about 65 percent and that psychoanalysis is beneficial about 83 percent of the time, as compared to "spontaneous" cures occurring at about a level of 30 percent.

There clearly are differences in the quality of the studies making up these summary statistics, but the better-designed ones, which employ control groups, lead to the overall conclusion that psychotherapy has "modestly positive effects." Researchers working in the area today generally agree that the broad question "Does psychotherapy work?" is of little further interest. More appropriately, we need to ask what specific kinds of intervention, by which specific therapists, are most effective in which ways, for which kinds of individuals, under what circumstances.

Let's look at some of the research designed to address these more specific issues and see if any of the findings might cast some light on the probable effects of the est training. The client-centered therapy of Carl Rogers does not have much in common with the est training at the level of *techniques* of change, but it does share a certain similarity to much of the est material hinting at a definition of the "ideal" personality or positive mental health. Rogers has specified that his view of good mental health includes self-actualization, self-esteem that is not qualified by ifs-ands-or-buts, openness to experience, personal growth, and a consistency between your "ideal" self and the self you feel you really are. A typical piece of research stemming from a Rogerian orientation shows that there was a discrepancy between "real" self and "ideal" self before counseling. After Rogerian therapy, people saw themselves as being much more like the self that they wanted to be. The increase in this similarity between real and ideal was highly significant, compared to appropriate control groups.

From the behaviorist perspective, studies have compared the relative effects of "real life" experiences to the effects of imaginary ones which, when accompanied by systematic relaxation instructions, have resulted in lessening or eliminating certain specific fears. These techniques bear an interesting similarity to some of the est exercises, or processes, in which fearful images are evoked from trainees who have entered a meditative state. There is evidence to suggest that "imaginal desensitization" is at least as effective as, and perhaps more effective than, actually girding one's loins to experience feared situations in reality.

The use of "punishment" in the est training was illustrated in Part I by accounts of the est trainer's making disparaging comments to trainees or calling them names which are generally viewed as insults. It is interesting that the research literature on the effects of punishment has demonstrated one major flaw: The results are not long-lasting. Therapeutic success may be seen initially but disappears gradually when treatment stops. Whatever the effects of "punishment" on est trainees, a large number of trainees continue to participate in est seminars or events after their graduation from the standard training. A high rate of continuing participation would be expected to prolong *whatever* effects accompanied the initial training.

The est training takes place in a group setting. How does research on group therapy help us assess the effects of est? A recent study of the effect of encounter groups by Lieberman and others has already become a classic in the field, partly because it investigated a phenomenon of wide popular interest and partly because it represents a very sophisticated application of the principles of research design.

The authors studied ten different varieties of encounter groups, including T-groups, Gestalt therapy groups, psychodrama, psychoanalytically oriented groups, transactional analysis groups, a bodily awareness group, marathon groups, personal growth groups, leaderless groups guided by tapes of encounter techniques, and a group based on the Synanon "game." Although these groups were defined largely by the labels attached to their presumed theoretical orientations, one of the major findings of the study was the relative uselessness of making such identifications. The benefit or harm that was experienced by members of the group was not related to the labels or the theoretical orientations of the groups but rather was very *directly related* to the behavior of the group leaders, regardless of the ideology they claimed. A wide variety of studies of therapists practicing individual as well as group forms of therapy confirms that the personal qualities of the therapist, or the behavior of the leader or trainer, are at least as important as the theory which is thought to underlie his or her work, and perhaps more so.

Adherents of encounter-group methods have often claimed that the effects of the group experience do not show up immediately but take some time to appear. I have heard that at least one est trainer suggests such a possibility to trainees. The Lieberman study suggests that this phenomenon of "late blooming" is fairly rare. Among those who showed no change at the conclusion of the group experiences investigated in this research, only 10 percent demonstrated signs of benefit six months later, while another 10 to 20 percent changed in the *opposite* direction, showing *less benefit* after the six-month interval. For all the groups included in this study, the average benefit rate was about 30 percent. That is not an impressive figure, especially when it is compared to the 30 percent rate of spontaneous remission cited earlier.

While the consensus of informed opinion, based on summaries of research findings, is that interventions similar to the est training have only modestly positive effects, I think that the existing research provides us with an *underestimate* of the effects of the est training. This training represents a distillation of some of the most powerful techniques and central precepts for attitude and behavior change. None of them are unique to est, but the package is an impressive one. I would guess that the effects of the est training are substantial for a large proportion of people. The effects may also be transient, although the large proportion of trainees continuing to participate in est events certainly suggests that this group of people would experience a continuation of whatever "effects" est had for them.

Should we completely discount the testimonials of est graduates, knowing that they are not sufficiently rigorous measures to qualify as scientific evidence? I don't think so. The fact that positive testimonials are so readily obtained from est graduates, in combination with the observation that a majority of people who take the est training continue to participate in est events, strongly suggests that participants have found the est experience to be rewarding. Even if "objective" changes are not documented in people's lives, it is noteworthy if people *feel* happier, more satisfied, more relaxed, and more "alive." If you *feel* happier, then you *are* happier—objective circumstances notwithstanding. Subjective states are clearly an important component of our lives.

The mechanism known as the "self-fulfilling prophecy" is also likely to embellish the feelings of positive results from the est training. If people feel increases in self-esteem, they may for example show greater self-confidence in their behavior and be more outgoing, assertive, and exuberant in their relations with other people. The reactions of others may be convincing demonstrations that life is indeed "working." It might also be that people are increasingly able to cope with the trials and tribulations of everyday life when they have self-confidence and a sense that "all's right with the world."

Despite the lack of scientific evidence as to the effects of the est training, it is clear to me that a substantial proportion of people exposed to it find it to be of value in their lives. As in the case of psychotherapy research, however, we need to go beyond the overall question of "Does est work?" Specifically, we need to define the meaning of the word "work." What specific changes occur in mood, self-concept, and performance in a variety of areas? Do physiological changes accompany people's perceptions that they are less anxious or stressed? It would also be important to ask whether certain kinds of people are more likely to be affected than others. Do particular personality characteristics increase or decrease the probability of change? Does being at a particular point in one's life make a difference? Does it make a difference if your friends or family also are est graduates? Does it make a difference if you have been through other forms of self-improvement programs or psychotherapy? If changes *are* brought about in the lives of some people, we would also want to find out what aspects of the est training were responsible for the changes. Does it matter who the trainer is? Does it matter if you do the training in your hometown? Are all the "rules" necessary to produce effects?

Research enabling us to answer these kinds of questions seems clearly justified, in view of the increasing popularity of est (as well as of other self-improvement activities) and the enthusiastic reports by participants. Given the expense of traditional forms of psychotherapy, and the limited sectors of the population in need that are actually reached by mental health services, a mass movement psychotherapeutic intervention clearly has enormous possibilities —if it "works."

15

Can est Be Harmful to Your Mental Health?

Is EST STRESSFUL? It almost has to be. Mere attendance at the two weekend sessions and the three weeknight seminars that are the format of the standard training requires many changes in one's way of life. When I was going through the training I changed my eating habits, sleeping habits, and smoking habits. I gave up leisure-time activities for those two weeks because I didn't have any leisure time. I changed my usual patterns of seeing and talking with family and friends. These changes in and of themselves qualify as stress. In addition, specific aspects of the training itself were stressful for many people: having to adhere to extensive rules and follow instructions, standing on a stage in front of a large audience, participating in activities that in other situations might be considered embarrassing, having important beliefs challenged or basic values questioned.

A popular research topic is the association between stress and the development of illness. This association has been observed in the case of physical illnesses such as coronary heart disease. The same association has been observed for illnesses that are called psychosomatic, such as peptic ulcer, essential hypertension, colitis, or asthma. The association with stress has also been observed for psychological disorders, such as depression, extreme anxiety, and various "nervous" conditions.

A growing number of recent research studies have accumulated evidence showing a relation between stressful life events and subsequent illness. Some life events are obviously stressful, or would be considered so by most of us: such major unwanted changes in our lives as the death of a loved one, a serious personal injury, divorce, being fired from work, being sent to prison. There are also many other smaller-scale life events which most of us recognize as entailing some stress or requiring us to make some readjustments in our lives: moving to a new city or a new neighborhood, retiring from work, changing schools or jobs, having a son or daughter or brother or sister leave home, experiencing difficulties in our relationships with people with whom we live or work.

Some of the early research on life events and the development of illness reported a surprising finding. It seemed as though life changes ordinarily seen as positive or desirable ones, such as getting married, being promoted at work, or improving one's financial situation, were related to increases in illness just as failures, losses, or disappointments were. Researchers understood this to mean that any occurrence which requires a significant change in an individual's usual life pattern involves some stress. A number of such events occurring together or following closely upon one another were significantly associated with the onset of illness. There is some argument among scientists over whether desirable life changes are related to illness in the same manner as undesirable ones are. The most recent research suggests that different kinds of events have different kinds of effects on the development of illness. Despite these complexities, we can still place some reliance on the major conclusion that it is *change itself* that causes stress by drawing upon our abilities to adapt and cope. For some people, the stress involved in the est training might just be the straw that breaks the camel's back.

There's also another side to it. Stress is not necessarily harmful. Some psychologists have suggested, with some evidence to back them up, that each of us has a characteristic level of what they call "arousal," a concept similar to excitement. Things are fine when our lives are proceeding in such a way as to keep us at the level which represents an optimal balance for us. When something changes, either to take us *above* that level *or below it*, we need to take some action to bring our lives back in line or problems may occur. For people whose everyday lives may have become a bit humdrum, routine, or lacking in variety, the changes and excitement involved in taking the est training may be just what they need to get back to that level which is best for them.

A related concept, also extensively researched, is that of anxiety. In common usage, the word "anxiety" has a certain negative sense and usually refers to an undesirable experience. It has been known for a long time, however, that a moderate amount of anxiety can be a useful thing and can actually result in improvements in performance on a wide variety of tasks. Students taking tests, for example, will do best if they are moderately anxious; those who have too little anxiety and those who experience too much will not do as well. In much the same manner, the est training may invigorate some people, who then may feel a burst of energy and enthusiasm that suddenly allows them to tackle things they've been procrastinating about for months.

Is there any additional scientific data on which to base an opinion as to the potential harmful effects of the est training? Some relevant research comes from the investigations of the effects of other forms of psychotherapy referred to in the preceding chapter.

In the Lieberman study of encounter groups, one of the groups investigated was a Synanon group. The

Synanon techniques were originally developed to find an effective means of helping drug addicts, a group of patients for whom the more traditional forms of psychotherapy were thought to be especially ineffective. Synanon eventually broadened its aims, however, and has no rules about the nature of the "problems" one has to claim in order to participate. In the Synanon group studied by Lieberman, nine or ten members were experienced Synanon participants; ten additional members were college students randomly assigned to participate in this group, as in each of the other groups under study, for research purposes.

The main factor that distinguishes the Synanon approach from that of other encounter groups is an emphasis on confrontation of a very particular sort. The assumption underlying this technique seems to be that undergoing the experience of being verbally attacked results in breaking down defenses in order to reach real feelings. This process is referred to as the Synanon "game," and it is a game in which the stakes are high. The attacks are aimed at discovering the weakest spots of the group members and uncovering their "phoniness," which generally refers to their psychopathology. The similarity to the est trainer's aggressive exposures of a trainee's "number" or "racket" is striking.

In the Lieberman study, the Synanon group had one of the highest psychological casualty rates. (A psychological casualty in this study was defined as referring to those people who, as a direct result of the group experience, develop significantly higher levels of psychological distress or who function in a less adaptive manner than before the experience.) I have of course heard stories of so-called est "casualties," people who experienced severe psychological distress while going through the training. I know of more than one psychotherapist treating such patients. There has been at least one legal action filed on behalf of someone claiming psychological damage as a result of the est training. In the training sessions which I attended, one of the participants spoke to me about a friend who had "flipped out" between the first and second week and was then in the process of obtaining psychiatric care. But it is essential to remember that, from a scientific point of view, there is no way we can say that these problems were a direct result of the est training. They may have been totally unrelated and coincidental, or the stress of the est training may just have been the last in a series of stressful events that had gradually taken their toll on the people involved.

There are no published scientific data on the incidence of acute psychological problems among people taking the est training. As we saw in chapter 14, it is extremely difficult to prove that any behavior, including feelings and self-reports of states of mind, is a *direct result* of any one factor. That is the reason why control groups are used in psychological research, to provide a group against which the changes in the group being researched can be measured. This would allow you to say, for example, that a certain percentage of people might have psychotic episodes anyway. Casualties that are correlated with taking the est training are not necessarily caused by it, any more than a correlation between the number of churches and the number of bars in a city means that churches cause bars or bars cause churches. Both churches and bars are *caused* by a third factor.

There are clearly additional influences on the relation between adverse reactions and taking the est training. It may be, for example, that a selection factor is operating and it is just those very people who are having difficulty or facing serious problems in their lives who are the ones who sign up for the est training, in numbers out of proportion to their numbers in the general population. It seems likely that many people take the est training, as they would go to encounter groups or any of the other self-improvement or consciousness-expanding experiences available in today's world, because they are in need of psychiatric assistance and hope they will find solutions to their problems in this manner.

The attractiveness of phenomena such as the est training seems to be related to an almost "something for nothing" appeal or at the very least a promise or a hope of gaining a great deal for what is, in relative terms, a fairly small investment, at least when compared to the cost both in time and money of more traditional forms of psychotherapy. Martin Gardner in *The New York Review of Books* has summed up such quests as the search for strawberry shortcut. It may well be that people who believe their lives can be "transformed" in two weekends, who have a need or desire for instant insight, who have not met with success in traditional forms of therapy or who perhaps have been too afraid or "defensive" to explore their psyches with members of the professional community, are precisely the people who are most prone to the "negative therapeutic reaction."

A similar selection factor is known to influence the occurrence of adverse reactions to some of the more widely used psychoactive drugs. (An adverse reaction in this context is defined specifically for purposes of measurement and refers to an intense anxiety experience which entails some or all of the following: recurring terrible thoughts or feelings, fear of loss of control, fear of permanent insanity, fear of impending death, despair, suicidal thoughts or wishes.) Recent research by Murray Naditch, a psychologist at Cornell University, has shown that people who use marijuana or LSD for the purpose of solving their problems (as compared to use for pleasure or curiosity) are more likely to have adverse reactions or "bad trips." It seems clear from this research that the *mo-*

tives one has for doing something can be a major influence on the manner in which that experience turns out. The research on marijuana and LSD also shows that psychological factors underlie the choice of motive. People who have underlying psychological problems are more likely to want to use marijuana for problem-solving purposes because (1) they have more problems and (2) they have fewer capacities with which to cope effectively with problems.

This is certainly not to say that most people who take the est training do so for such problem-solving reasons. It should be remembered, however, from the description in chapter 2 of the procedures for enrolling in the est training that "pleasure" or "curiosity" are evidently reasons unacceptable to the training registrars. Enrollees are "encouraged" to commit themselves to results such as becoming less anxious or clearing up relationships with important people in their lives. This "encouragement" is supplemented by the leverage of being unable to get into the training room until one's questionnaire responses are considered satisfactory to the gatekeeper. Even though many people may write down such reasons under protest, there must be at least another sizable group who had such reasons initially or came to have them in the process of registering. For people who take the training for such reasons, the probability of adverse reactions is increased.

Even in such cases, however, it would be extremely difficult to sort out the factors influencing psychological casualties when and if they occur. Very sophisticated research designs are necessary to sort out all the relevant possibilities. These might be people, for example, who would have "broken down" sooner or later anyway. In addition, there is at least some opinion in the psychotherapeutic community that such "breakdowns" are not necessarily disasters but may in fact be the start of a process of reconstitution that will eventually result in improvements in mental health and in higher levels of functioning for these people than they were previously capable of when they had painful feelings bottled up inside. If the est training is for some people the proximal cause in a long chain of events leading toward expressions of psychological distress or a breakdown in functioning, it may nevertheless be ultimately "useful" in that it facilitates that person's getting the professional treatment that he or she has long been in need of but has nevertheless managed, perhaps at great cost, to avoid.

Since much of the content of the est training might reasonably be characterized as confrontational in nature, it is worth considering the findings of the Lieberman study of encounter groups in slightly more detail, with particular emphasis on the negative results stemming from the Synanon group, which emphasized confrontation and attack. When compared to the other groups studied, the Synanon group had one of the highest rates of people dropping out before the sessions were ended. There is no publicly available data on the drop-out rate from est. Nor will there be any (of a quality acceptable as scientific evidence) until independent researchers have been permitted to conduct and publish rigorously designed studies with appropriate controls.

Although we know there is a high drop-out rate from Synanon-type confrontation groups, that of course does not mean that a comparably high drop-out rate would be predicted in the est training with its similar confrontational tactics. In the Lieberman study, the students who were assigned to participate in the Synanon group were volunteers in a research project. Although they probably wished to cooperate with the researchers, these students nevertheless presumably had made little personal investment in or commitment to the group experience. They were thus relatively free of internally generated pressure against dropping out. They were undoubtedly free of external pressure from the researchers, who were bound by the ethics of scientific research to have participation in the study be truly "voluntary." The psychological forces against dropping out of est are immeasurably greater. People have spent $250 and incurred other costs to their time and personal convenience. You don't just "not show up" for your next scheduled session of the est training, without receiving phone calls from the volunteers at the est office. It has been reported that many people find these "follow-ups" to be quite persistent in nature. A member of my training group told me that she had been told that she "created" the flu which was her reason for staying home and missing a session. She reported to me that she was also told that she could "disappear" her symptoms if she took responsibility for her illness. Another member of my training group (described in chapter 3) had been told that his decision not to return to the training after experiencing the first installment was definitive proof that he was an asshole. It is clear that these are tactics of high-pressure salesmanship specifically designed to increase the difficulty of making a decision to drop out. Given the susceptibility of many or even most people to such tactics, in combination with the probably even more powerful influence of their own previous commitment to the training, we could predict that the drop-out rates in est would be substantially lower than in those situations where withdrawal from a treatment situation is an unpressured choice. Were the est "follow-up" not quite so extensive or the situation designed in such a manner that people did not make such intensive personal investments in the training, we might expect that drop-out rates would be fairly high and reasonably comparable to the drop-out rates in other groups utilizing confrontational tactics.

In the Lieberman study, those members who completed the Synanon group without dropping out gave it at the end a rating as a positive experience that was about average for all the groups under study. This average rating, however, was composed of two groups of people, each with reactions at one extreme or the other. Half of the people thought the group had been an extremely positive experience for them and half thought it had been extremely negative. Considering all the groups included in the Lieberman study, the people who experienced negative results in combination with the psychological casualties constituted about 19 percent of the total. That is, for 19 percent or close to one out of five people who participated in these group experiences, the results were "harmful." This is quite a high figure and should be viewed in comparison to the 30-percent benefit rate from groups as reported in chapter 14.

There is also substantial research, including a large number of studies with appropriate controls, showing that psychological casualties occur not only in groups but also in individual psychotherapy. This is referred to as the "deterioration effect" and has been estimated to occur in about 10 percent of individual psychotherapy patients. It is important to stress that the studies on which these data were based were in all cases studies of professionally trained psychotherapists who had been through many selection procedures designed to weed out the less competent members of the profession. The point here is merely to note that the generally accepted figure of 10 percent of patients "getting worse" or deteriorating in individual psychotherapy would in all likelihood be much higher than that, were the psychotherapists on whose work this research was based not subject to the rigorous screening, supervision, and review which are part of any legitimate course of preparation to practice psychotherapy.

The research on this deterioration effect in psychotherapy provides some explanations of the circumstances under which deterioration or adverse reactions to psychotherapy occur. Much of this research has focused on attributes of the therapists and then related these therapist characteristics to the improvement or deterioration of patients. These studies show that patient deterioration is most likely when therapists lack empathy, warmth, and genuineness. Therapists who make evaluative statements frequently in therapy are more likely to have patients who deteriorate rather than improve. Another series of studies has shown that therapists who lack warmth, empathy, and genuineness are also likely to be confrontational, especially in confronting a patient's liabilities. The existence of the "psychonoxious" therapist is well accepted in the clinical research literature. I wonder how est trainers would score on measures of warmth, empathy, genuineness, and avoiding confrontation of trainees' liabilities or weaknesses.

There are some additional considerations in looking at the potential of est to cause psychological harm. For intensive group therapy on an outpatient basis, it is reasonable to decide that patients exhibiting such characteristics as paranoia, pronounced narcissism, suicidal tendencies, or sociopathy (to a trained diagnostician or on a standard test) would be poor candidates for this kind of treatment.

Even though the specific issues might be different for therapists of different theoretical orientations, any legitimate therapist will evaluate the suitability of a potential patient for a specific type of therapy. As a psychoanalytically oriented psychotherapist, I would make a careful assessment of a patient's psychological state before beginning treatment or before deciding what manner of treatment was appropriate in a particular case. Among other things, I would pay special attention to the patient's capacity to tolerate anxiety, knowing that some increase in anxiety is an almost inevitable accompaniment of therapeutic progress; if the patient seemed vulnerable to being overwhelmed by anxiety-producing stimuli, I would not consider him or her to be an appropriate candidate for psychoanalytic, insight-oriented therapy intended to "uncover" previously repressed or unconscious material. I would also consider carefully the nature and quality of the patient's characteristic mechanisms of defense, to find out how extensive they were and how rigidly or flexibly they were used. I would want to know if the patient had substantial pent-up aggression, the release of which might not be tolerated in the slow, carefully titrated, and highly verbal manner appropriate to verbal psychotherapy. I would want to know if the patient was capable of enduring a substantial amount of frustration of his or her basic drives, in order to be capable of analyzing this material rather than acting it out. And I would be specially attuned to any indications that the patient might be psychotic or in that borderline category where psychosis as a *result* of therapy can be expected if the therapist does not modify his or her techniques appropriately. These are only a few examples of the kinds of questions I would ask before beginning psychoanalytic psychotherapy with anyone. Therapists of other persuasions would have a different list, or would perhaps use different language or concepts to express many of the same concerns, but it would certainly be the case that any responsible therapist would at least want to make similar determinations before beginning treatment, for these issues form some of the most basic assumptions on which currently accepted therapeutic practice proceeds.

There is no opportunity in the est training for such determinations to be made by the trainers. Even had they the opportunity, they lack the professional competence and the legal right to do so, given current laws regulating the practice of psychodiagnosis and psychotherapy.

What selection procedures are used to screen people for the est training? On the application form, they ask if you have ever been hospitalized for "psychiatric care or a mental disorder." They ask if you are now, or have been, in therapy. They ask, for those in therapy now or recently, if you are "winning" in therapy. They provide on the application form the name and telephone number of a physician on their staff who may be contacted by your therapist to obtain additional information about the training. They ask you to sign a statement, if you are in therapy, that you have advised your therapist that you are taking the est training. I have heard that they strongly discourage people who have had psychiatric hospitalizations or who have not "won" in therapy from taking the est training; an announcement to that effect was made in the training sessions I attended. I have also heard that in many cases, according to criteria I have no knowledge of, they request certain people to obtain a therapist's permission before taking the training. A former colleague of mine who is a psychiatrist was asked to make such a determination and also to sign a statement that he would be available for consultation during the period the person seeking this approval was going through the training (and presumably for some period thereafter).

These precautions are certainly admirable and

appropriate. But are they sufficient? Do they cover persons who intentionally or because of incapacity misrepresent their psychiatric status on the application form? Or persons who feel that their medical or psychiatric history is not appropriately revealed to a private business offering them an "educational" service? Or the legions of people who have serious psychopathology but who have never sought, or who have avoided seeking, professional treatment? Are the est selection procedures in any manner comparable to the hours of individual interview and screening tests conducted by a trained clinician under the supervision of an even more experienced member of the attending staff, that constitute the basic intake procedure at the better psychiatric outpatient clinics?

The point is this: Trainers in est do not and cannot take the precautions that would be considered appropriate for psychotherapy. They use techniques such as confrontation which undermine psychological defenses and strip away resistance. They use some techniques whose effect is to increase anxiety and other techniques which encourage regression to developmentally more primitive modes of functioning. There are only two logical possibilities as to the implications of such activities: (1) Based on currently accepted standards of psychotherapeutic practice, est uses techniques indiscriminately which in a certain proportion of the population are known to be harmful and potentially quite dangerous, *or* (2) based on the use of such techniques in est, if research were to indicate that no harm occurs, some of the most basic tenets of psychotherapy are lacking any basis in evidence.

Whichever possibility turns out to be accurate, and we will not know until the appropriate research has been conducted and then subjected to scrutiny by the scientific community, the implications in either case are nevertheless serious and profound.

16

Why est?

MANY PEOPLE HAVE QUESTIONS about the founder of est and the nature of the organization which stands behind the training in which so many have found so much. Critics of est that I have spoken with, heard, or read about focus on many different issues. Some are concerned about the implications of the transformation of Jack Rosenberg, also known as Jack Frost, also known as von Savage, now known as Werner Erhard, the guru of est. Some find his background as a salesman of cars and encyclopedias to be an inappropriate preparation for peddling happiness, love, health, and self-expression.

If the training has value for people, does it matter that Erhard the packager has dubious credentials? As one of the est graduates I interviewed said, "If I've been brainwashed, I'd like to know who's got his hands on the soap."

Other critics point to the nature of the est organi-

173

zation, which is secretive, suspicious, and vigilant. Jesse Kornbluth, writing in *New Times* magazine, describes the organization's questionable financing arrangements, the fifteen-page security memos, the hiring of private detectives to "interview" people who have talked with reporters. An internal memorandum from a staff member to the president of the est corporation describes plans to "handle" certain psychologists and psychiatrists who have been publicly critical of est. The second page of the memo refers to an est trainee who was hospitalized. The writer of the memo says he intended to call her to get the name of her psychiatrist at Stanford so that he could be closed off as a source of rumors about est. It may well be satisfaction and aliveness that such activities are intended to serve; it clearly is not candor and freedom.

A woman in Hawaii took the est training and said she suffered severe psychological distress, for which she sought psychiatric care. She brought suit against est of Hawaii, Inc., for the damages she suffered, claiming that the training constituted unauthorized practice of psychology. Interrogatories were presented to defendant Werner Erhard, who answered in a characteristic estian style. When asked about "harmful, negative, or adverse reactions" to the training, his reply in part was that any answer would be inaccurate because " 'Harmful, negative, or adverse reaction' is a subjective concept." That's an interesting answer from someone whose views on the nature of subjective reality are being sold to thousands of people at $250 a head. It is particularly interesting that the concept of "adverse reaction" seems "subjective" to Erhard; the concept is not too subjective for the *Journal of Abnormal Psychology*, an official publication of the American Psychological Association, which has published several scientific articles quantifying it.

In the same set of interrogatories, Erhard was asked, "Did you, before the administration of the training, tell plaintiff what techniques, processes, or procedures would be employed in the training?"

His reply, in part: "No. The question cannot be answered because nothing is administered."

This answer has a certain Zen cuteness to it. While inscrutability may be charming in the temples of est, it is usually not seen as facilitating the purpose of the discovery process in a court of law.

When I reflect upon the contents of the est training, I find it difficult to separate it from disturbing revelations about the founder of est and the nature of the organization. I'm not advocating the philosophical principle that the value of a precept or a theory rests on the quality of the person espousing it. I *am* suggesting that there is a consistency between the implications of the est training and the manner in which the est organization is run. The obfuscation in the est training, the quick sidestep to avoid confronting an issue that is the heart of the estian shift, the exhortation to "transcend your mind," to move away from reasonableness into an estian definition of "enlightenment"—all have the same appeal and the same danger. The danger *is* the appeal.

Why is est capturing a ground swell of interest among America's more successful classes? Its anti-intellectualism is a standard piece of apple pie. On the recent political scene, both Spiro Agnew and George Wallace struck a responsive chord with their appeals to ignorance and non-think. In a nation on the make there has always been a premium on the quick answer. The misplaced optimism motivating eight years of promises that we could see the light at the end of the tunnel in Southeast Asia is totally consistent with the promise of two weekends to enlightenment. McDonald's hamburgers may have their culinary critics, but the critics haven't stopped the sale of 18 billion all-beef patties on sesame seed buns. We like it fast and we like it simple. And we resent those who make demands upon our critical capacities.

Another common theme in analyses of the American character has dealt with the need for community. The factors depriving us of authentic social support have been extensively reiterated: technological change, social and geographic mobility, the individualistic search for self-aggrandizement, competitiveness, and the emphasis on getting the job done at the expense of fulfilling human needs. All these factors separate us from friends, family, partners, and community. The desperate need to belong to something larger than oneself has constantly been assaulted by the gradual erosion of social and religious institutions. Economic institutions are no longer sensible repositories for faith. The culmination of the loss of credibility in political institutions occurred with the retching upheaval needed to cleanse our collective selves of the infection symbolized by Watergate. There are no more institutions standing *in loco parentis*. We are orphans.

Est fills the gap. It holds us in parental arms and gives us brothers and sisters to play with. The shared experiences of the training clearly increase the sense of affiliation trainees have with one another. They have bared their burdens and shared their sins. They'll never be lonely again.

This family is a classic, patriarchal and autocratic. The training is a precisely articulated series of manipulations carefully designed to produce the desired effects. One of the effects is dependency, a dependency that approaches infantilization. The trainer tells you when to talk, when to eat, when to drink, when to applaud, when to sit, and when to stand.

The authoritarianism of the training is a beginner's course in the totalitarianism you will be subject to if you join the est organization. According to Kornbluth, staff members report their sexual activities to Erhard as though he were an investigator from the Board of Health trying to limit the spread of venereal disease. Every staff member submits compulsory "Notes to Werner" on a designated day of the month, depending on the initial of his or her last name. This is no casual office suggestion box. Staff members are instructed to type or neatly print their notes, using two sides of the page on a special "Notes to Werner" pad. Notes are due at an assigned hour and day of each month, covering, in consecutive order, seven items including "If there's anything you are not saying, say that" and "If there's anything you don't want to say, say that." It's a grown-up version of Truth or Consequences. Kornbluth's astute analysis of the ultimate triviality and obsessiveness of the leaders of est suggests the nature of the glue that binds the training to the organization.

The appeal of dependency is no surprise in an era when personal independence has been a watchword. Shakespeare anticipated by about three centuries Freud's insight into the defensive nature of bravado: "The lady doth protest too much, methinks." So our festering need for dependency, so unacceptable to express and satisfy in our day-to-day lives, finds gratification in the womb of est. In the training, one can regress to the earliest phases of life. The trainer will feed you with emotional supplies, the nutritional content of which is certified by the conversions of other trainees. The Good Mother of one's most private fantasies has been made real. The symbolic meaning of the entire est training is concretized in one of the final processes, where trainees actually create and in their imaginations sculpt the body of a man and woman who will join them in their "centers." The oral supplies of this mother are not made available as a free lunch; she's a vending machine like all the rest—you need a coin to get the breast. The price of obtaining her nurturance is surrender of autonomy to the all-controlling Father. The est trainees, in their "agreements," have contracted for dependency upon the trainer for the very definition of reality. In the seventieth hour or so of the training, worn down by fatigue, buoyed up by the promise of ultimate salvation, you "get it."

The dependency is not lacking in purpose. It is promoted as a mechanism for selling a point of view. The come-on is nearly irresistible. "Don't believe anything I say," says the trainer, miring us in an age-old philosophical swamp. If we accept his invitation to the dance of disbelief, we must also disbelieve his disclaimer, which spins the circle round again and leaves us at—belief.

The seduction has an enormous appeal. "Fairy tales can come true, it can happen to you, if you're young at heart." And very young indeed; what the surrender buys us is the narcissistic omnipotence of infantile fantasies. The infinite power we obtain is real, and it works, but it is a Pyrrhic success. As C. S. Lewis has told us, miracles *do* happen—but only to those who believe in them. The power of est sustains us in our imaginations only so long as we pay daily devotion to the household gods of our family romance. The trainer *or* Werner *or* the training are parental imagoes, idealized and enshrined. The est point of view *must* invalidate those of others in order to sustain its monotheistic appeal.

No wonder people can't explain why the training turns them on. The explanation would be the ultimate embarrassment. Also, once understood, the estian conversion and its accompanying behaviors would be stripped of their ability to provide the gratification which caused and maintained them.

But est is not a one-note tune. The training offers other nourishment for the ravenous psyches of our time. The appeal of the cathartic release that occurs both in the "sharing" and in the est "processes" is based on the existence of something to cathart. There's no question that trainees arrive carrying the baggage of pent-up emotion. Some of us travel light with a mere attaché case full of collected grievances; others need trucks full of steamer trunks to contain the injuries of their pasts. But the differences among us are only of degree. We've all paid our dues and come by our problems legitimately.

The guilt-inducing child-rearing techniques of the middle class are well known. Growing up involves a succession of frustrations. Frustration almost universally arouses the response of aggression. For society to function, aggression is kept in check. Aggression turned inward is guilt, inextricably linked to the depression which is nearly epidemic in contemporary society. The whole society invites punishment. Those who have failed require punishment for the anger which their failure generates; those who succeed require punishment for the guilt their success engenders. There's something in est for everyone. The ones who turn their aggression inward are allowed the masochistic pleasure of being on the receiving end of the trainer's thrusts. Those who sit back as voyeurs obtain the vicarious sadistic gratifications of their identification with the aggressor. The erotization of aggressive impulses that has reached its culmination in the current sex and murder fantasies of "snuff" pornography is cleaned up a bit in the est act, but not so much as to deprive the audience of perverse satisfaction.

These est graduates have been too modest in sharing their experiences of the training. The "satisfaction" they report is a euphemism; what the training produces is an intense, orgasmic euphoria.

Isn't it worth all this, though, to make the world work? The more I envision the goose-stepping corps at the center of the est organization, the more virtue I see in anarchy. The last person who made the trains run on time participated in the creation of a nightmare. The only way to stop a nightmare is to wake up.

References

CHAPTER 10.   Is est Brainwashing?

Readers interested in brainwashing may find further information in the following sources: W. Sargant, *Battle for the Mind* (Garden City, N.Y.: Doubleday & Co., 1957); E. H. Schein, *Coercive Persuasion* (New York: W. W. Norton & Co., 1961); R. J. Lifton, *Thought Reform and the Psychology of Totalism: A Study of "Brainwashing" in China* (New York: W. W. Norton & Co., 1961); and A. D. Biderman, Social-psychological needs and "involuntary" behavior as illustrated by compliance in interrogation, *Sociometry*, 23 (1960), 120–47.

Page 117.   "In an article in *Psychology Today*": *See* M. Brewer, Erhard Seminars Training: 'We're gonna tear you down and put you back together,' *Psychology Today*, August, 1975.

Page 118.   . . . "social psychologist Philip Zimbardo": *See* P. Zimbardo and F. L. Ruch, *Psychology and Life*, 9th ed. (Glenview, Ill.: Scott, Foresman and Company, 1975), p. 585.

Page 120. "... well-known principles of attitude and behavior change": There is an extensive social-psychological literature on these topics. Interested readers might consult L. Festinger, *A Theory of Cognitive Dissonance* (Stanford, Cal.: Stanford University Press, 1957); J. W. Brehm and A. R. Cohen, *Explorations in Cognitive Dissonance* (New York: John Wiley & Sons, 1962); and C. I. Hovland, I. L. Janis, and H. H. Kelley, *Communication and Persuasion* (New Haven, Conn.: Yale University Press, 1953).

"... the 'foot-in-the-door-technique' ": *See* J. L. Freedman and S. C. Fraser, Compliance without pressure: The foot-in-the-door technique, *Journal of Personality and Social Psychology*, 4 (1966), 195–202.

"... we *infer* our own feelings and attitudes.": *See* D. J. Bem, An experimental analysis of self-persuasion, *Journal of Experimental Social Psychology*, 1 (1965), 199–218.

Page 121*f*. "... the human need to justify our actions": *See* L. Festinger, *A Theory of Cognitive Dissonance* (Stanford, Cal.: Stanford University Press, 1957).

CHAPTER 12. Why Do They Train 250 People
at Once?

Page 130. "... a Frenchman named Le Bon": *See* G.
Le Bon, *The Crowd: A Study of the Popular Mind* (London: Unwin, 1896).

Page 131. "McDougall ... writing in 1920": *See* W.
McDougall, *The Group Mind* (New York:
G. P. Putnam's Sons, 1920).

"In a classic set of experiments, Solomon
Asch": *See* S. Asch, Effects of group pressure upon the modification and distortion
of judgment, in M. H. Guetzkow (ed.),
Groups, Leadership and Men (Pittsburgh:
Carnegie Press, 1951), pp. 117–90.

Page 132. "Other researchers interested in further investigation": *See* D. Krech, R. S. Crutchfield, and E. L. Ballachey, *Individual and
Society* (New York: McGraw-Hill, 1962).

CHAPTER 13. Why Won't They Let You Go
to the Bathroom?

Page 135. "Emotional arousal is thought to be": *See*
J. D. Frank, *Persuasion and Healing*, rev.
ed. (New York: Schocken Books, 1974).

Page 136. "According to William James": *See* W. J. James, *Principles of Psychology* (New York: Smith, 1890).

"Physiologist Walter Cannon": *See* W. B. Cannon, *Bodily Changes in Pain, Hunger, Fear and Rage*, 2nd ed. (New York: Appleton-Century-Crofts, 1929).

Page 137. "The extent of this influence": *See* S. Schachter and J. Singer, Cognitive, social, and physiological determinants of emotional state, *Psychological Review*, 69 (1962), 379–99.

Page 138. "The authority of the leader of a group": *See* C. I. Hovland, I. L. Janis, and H. H. Kelley, *Communication and Persuasion: Psychological Studies of Opinion Change* (New Haven, Conn.: Yale University Press, 1953).

". . . the development of faith in a healer": *See* J. D. Frank, *Persuasion and Healing.*

CHAPTER 14. Does est Work?

Page 144. "Psychological experimenters who have particular expectations": *See* R. Rosenthal, *Experimenter Effects in Behavioral Research* (New York: Appleton-Century-Crofts, 1966).

Page 145. "In a classic study of the effects": See F. J. Roethlisberger, W. J. Dickson, and H. A. Wright, *Management and the Worker: An Account of a Research Program Conducted by the Western Electric Company*, Mass.: Harvard University Press, 1939).

Page 146. "British psychologist Hans Eysenck": See H. J. Eysenck, The effects of psychotherapy, in H. J. Eysenck (ed.), *Handbook of Abnormal Psychology: An Experimental Approach* (New York: Basic Books, 1961), pp. 697-725.

Page 147. "These data have been superseded": See A. E. Bergin, The evaluation of therapeutic outcomes, in A. E. Bergin and S. L. Garfield (eds.), *Handbook of Psychotherapy and Behavior Change: An Empirical Analysis* (New York: John Wiley & Sons, 1971), pp. 217–70.

Page 148. "Rogers has specified that his view": See C. R. Rogers, *On Becoming a Person: A Therapist's View of Psychotherapy* (Boston: Houghton Mifflin Co., 1961).

"A typical piece of research": See J. M. Butler and G. V. Haigh, Changes in the relation between self-concepts and ideal concepts consequent upon client-centered counseling, in C. R. Rogers and R. F. Dymond (eds.), *Psychotherapy and Personality Change: Co-ordinated Research Studies in the Client-centered Approach* (Chicago: University of Chicago Press, 1954).

Page 148. "There is evidence to suggest that": *See* H. J. Eysenck and H. R. Beech, Counter conditioning and related methods. In A. E. Bergin and S. L. Garfield (eds.), *Handbook of Psychotherapy and Behavior Change: An Empirical Analysis* (New York: John Wiley & Sons, 1971), pp. 543–611.

Page 149. ". . . the research literature on the effects of punishment": *See* G. J. S. Wilde, Correspondence, *Behavior Research and Therapy*, 2 (1965), 313.

"A recent study of the effect of encounter groups": *See* M. A. Lieberman, I. D. Yalom, and M. B. Miles, *Encounter Groups: First Facts* (New York: Basic Books, 1973).

Page 150. ". . . studies of therapists": *See* C. B. Truax and R. R. Carkhuff, *Toward Effective Counseling and Psychotherapy: Training and Practice* (Chicago: Aldine Publishing Co., 1967).

CHAPTER 15.   Can est Be Harmful
                to Your Mental Health?

Page 155.   "A popular research topic": *See* B. S. Doh-
            renwend and B. P. Dohrenwend (eds.),
            Stressful Life Events (New York: John
            Wiley & Sons, 1974).

Page 156.   "There is some argument": *See* A. Vino-
            kur and M. Selzer, Desirable versus unde-
            sirable life events: Their relationship to
            stress and mental disease. *Journal of Per-
            sonality and Social Psychology*, 32 (1975),
            329–37.

            "Some psychologists have suggested": *See*
            D. W. Fiske and S. R. Maddi (eds.), *Func-
            tions of Varied Experience* (Homewood,
            Ill.: Dorsey Press, 1961).

Page 157.   "In the Lieberman study of encounter
            groups": *See* M. A. Lieberman, I. D. Yalom,
            and M. B. Miles, *Encounter Groups: First
            Facts* (New York: Basic Books, 1973).

Page 161.   "Recent research by Murray Naditch":
            See M. P. Naditch, Relation of motives for
            drug use and psychopathology in the de-
            velopment of acute adverse reactions to
            psychoactive drugs, *Journal of Abnormal
            Psychology*, 84 (1975), 374–485.

Page 166. "This is referred to as the deterioration effect": *See* A. E. Bergin, The evaluation of therapeutic outcomes, in A. E. Bergin and S. L. Garfield (eds.), *Handbook of Psychotherapy and Behavior Change: An Empirical Analysis* (New York: John Wiley & Sons, 1971), pp. 217–70.

Page 167. "Much of this research has focused": *See* C. B. Truax and K. M. Mitchell, Research on certain therapist interpersonal skills in relation to process and outcome, in Bergin and Garfield, *Psychotherapy and Behavior Change*, pp. 299–344.

"Another series of studies has shown": *See* B. G. Berenson, K. M. Mitchell, and R. Laney, Level of therapist functioning, types of confrontation, and type of patient, *Journal of Clinical Psychology*, 24 (1968), 111–13. *See also* B. G. Berenson, K. M. Mitchell, and J. A. Moravec, Level of therapist functioning, type of confrontation, and patient depth of self-exploration, *Journal of Counseling Psychology*, 15 (1968), 136–39.

"The existence of the 'psychonoxious' therapist": *See* C. B. Truax, Effective ingredients in psychotherapy: An approach to unraveling the patient-therapist interaction,

Journal of Counseling Psychology, 10 (1963), 256–63.

Page 168. "For intensive group therapy on an outpatient basis": *See* I. D. Yalom, *The Theory and Practice of Group Psychotherapy*, 2nd ed. (New York: Basic Books, 1975), p. 221.

CHAPTER 16. Why est?

Page 174. "Jesse Kornbluth, writing in *New Times* magazine": *See New Times*, March 19, 1976.

R00031 84837

600677

600677 SS

158   Fenwick, Sheridan, 1942-
                Getting it

795

18 SANDY SPRINGS

ATLANTA PUBLIC LIBRARY